Experiencing God

Experiencing God

Faith Narratives of Episcopalians

EDITED BY
Ian S. Markham
AND
Kimberly E. Dunn

FOREWORD BY
Katherine Sonderegger

CASCADE *Books* • Eugene, Oregon

EXPERIENCING GOD
Faith Narratives of Episcopalians

Cascade Books
An Imprint of Wipf and Stock Publishers
199 W. 8th Ave., Suite 3
Eugene, OR 97401

www.wipfandstock.com

PAPERBACK ISBN: 978-1-6667-7248-7
HARDCOVER ISBN: 978-1-6667-7249-4
EBOOK ISBN: 978-1-6667-7250-0

Cataloguing-in-Publication data:

Names: Markham, Ian S. [editor.] | Dunn, Kimberly E. [editor]. | Sonderegger,
Katherine [foreword writer].

Title: Experiencing God : faith narratives of Episcopalians / edited by Ian S.
Markham and Kimberly E. Dunn ; foreword by Katherine Sonderegger.

Description: Eugene, OR: Cascade Books, 2024 | Includes bibliographical refer-
ences.

Identifiers: ISBN 978-1-6667-7248-7 (paperback) | ISBN 978-1-6667-7249-4
(hardcover) | ISBN 978-1-6667-7250-0 (ebook)

Subjects: LCSH: Episcopal Church | Spiritual biography | Spirituality—Christi-
anity | Spirituality

Classification: BV4501 M37 2024 (paperback) | BV4501 (ebook)

VERSION NUMBER 03/22/24

Contents

Contributors

Santana Alvarado (they/them), known by their stage name Santana Sankofa, is a queer Afro-Caribbean singer/songwriter, educator, and organizer born and raised in Los Angeles with roots in New York who is currently living in Baltimore. Their art and activism centers on disrupting faith-based, political, and academic institutions; creating programs to activate youth; and empowering trans and queer people through the sounds and spaces they cultivate. Santana explores themes of justice, radical intimacy, and transforming fear into freedom on their newest album "Ashes" available on their website: santanasankofa.com.

The Rev. Canon Dr. Henry L. Atkins Jr. is a retired priest of the Diocese of New Jersey. Canon Atkins has worked in parishes, universities, seminaries, and with religious orders in both the United States and Latin America. He has served as a co-chair of the Episcopal Church's National Commission on Racism, as vice president of the Theological Education Commission for Latin America and the Caribbean and was a founding member of the Shalem Institute for Spiritual Formation. He presently lives with his wife, Lucy Treadwell, in Las Cruces, New Mexico, where he works in the field of Eco Theology with the Holy Cross Franciscans.

Dr. Linda Beatrice Brown is a retired professor of Black Literature and author of three published novels, two books of nonfiction and three volumes of poetry. She is a frequent lecturer on the topic of anti-racism. Her book, *Belles of Liberty*, chronicles her participation in the sixties sit-ins. She is currently on the faculty of the School at Space for Conscious Living, where she has led workshops on such topics as The Divine Feminine and Uncovering Patriarchy. Linda is a lifetime Episcopalian and longtime member of Holy Trinity Episcopal Church in Greensboro.

The Rev. Canon Lydia Bucklin is Canon to the Ordinary for Discipleship & Vitality at the Episcopal Diocese of Northern Michigan, a Church Strategy Consultant, and a Senior Advisor for the Mutual Ministry Initiative at Virginia Theological Seminary. Her expertise is in church leadership, collaborative ministry, and missional engagement.

The Rev. Kim L. Coleman, Rector and Senior Pastor of Trinity Episcopal Church in Arlington, Virginia, since November 2002, oversees Trinity's dynamic justice and outreach ministries, including an Anti-Human Trafficking Mission and Ministry Group, a Congregational Mental Health Initiative, TNT4RJ (an ecumenical racial justice and healing partnership between Trinity and NOVA Catholic Community), Trinity's international Mothers' Union affiliate, as well as the Columbia Pike Thrift Shop. A May 2001 cum laude graduate of Virginia Theological Seminary (VTS), Mother Kim's involvements beyond the parish have included serving as Diocesan Standing Committee and Executive Board member, Deputy to General Convention, Diocesan Chaplain for Episcopal Church Women, Diocesan Archdean (and Dean for the Arlington Region), Adjunct Professor at VTS, and VTS Alumnae Association Vice President. She is currently completing her second term (2022–2025) as National President of the Union of Black Episcopalians.

Kimberly E. Dunn is the Associate Rector of Saint Paul's Church in Augusta, Georgia. She is a graduate of Virginia Theological Seminary. She is a professional life coach and strategist. She holds a BM and MM in Music in Vocal Performance in Opera Theater and has been a professional international performer. She is a Daughter of the Order of the Daughters of the King and a member of Alpha Kappa Alpha Sorority, Inc.

The Rev. Brooks Graebner, PhD, is Rector Emeritus of St. Matthew's Episcopal Church in Hillsborough, North Carolina, and the Historiographer of the Episcopal Diocese of North Carolina. He holds degrees from the University of Virginia (BA), Duke University (MDiv and PhD), and the Virginia Theological Seminary (Certificate in Anglican Studies and DD). He is a former Director and Officer of the Historical Society of the Episcopal Church.

The Rev. J. Barney Hawkins IV is the director of the Bicentennial Celebration at Virginia Theological Seminary. Since 2000, he has served in a variety of capacities at Virginia Theological Seminary, including the Vice President for Institutional Advancement, Associate Dean of the Center for Anglican Communion Studies, and Professor of Pastoral Theology. A specialist on eighteenth-century Anglicanism in the American colonies, he spent more than two decades in parish ministry. He is the author and editor of several books, including *Episcopal Etiquette and Ethics*.

The Rev. Dr. Ian S. Markham is the dean and president of Virginia Theological Seminary and the president of The General Theological Seminary and professor of theology and ethics. With degrees from King's College London, the University of Cambridge, and the University of Exeter, he has worked at Liverpool Hope University and Hartford Seminary before moving to Alexandria, Virginia. He is the author of numerous books and is priest associate at St. Paul's Episcopal Church in Alexandria, Virginia.

The Rev. **Timothy Patterson** received a BA from Duke University, MDiv from Duke Divinity School, and completed Anglican studies at General Theological Seminary. He has experience working with autistic young people, serving as a Hospice volunteer, and working as a psychiatric counselor. Ordained as a priest in 1990, was called as rector of Holy Trinity Church in Greensboro, North Carolina, at the end of 1996. Timothy served as ordained clergy for over thirty years. As a leader in ecumenical ministries in the community, Tim was a primary founder of the Guilford Regional AIDS Interfaith Network (now Higher Ground), The Barnabas Network, and The Servant Leadership School of Greensboro. Tim's wife, Kathleen Forbes, is an educational administrator at UNCG.

The Rev. **Altagracia Pérez-Bullard, PhD**, is the director of contextual ministry and assistant professor of practical theology at Virginia Theological Seminary in Alexandria. Altagracia has served in ministry over thirty years as youth minister, community leader, and priest. Dr. Pérez-Bullard has brought leadership to the issues of HIV/AIDS, youth violence, worker justice and living wage, health disparities in communities of color, housing, and community empowerment. In each of these areas, she has sought to build bridges and create alliances between communities across lines of difference.

The Rt. Rev. **Rayford Jeffrey Ray** was consecrated the eleventh bishop of the Episcopal Diocese of Northern Michigan in 2010 and is a four-time deputy to the General Convention. He earned a BA degree in history and language arts from Cameron University in Lawton, Oklahoma, and a graduate of Nashotah House. He is married to Suzanne Ray, also a priest in the diocese of Northern Michigan.

The Rev. **C. K. Robertson, PhD**, has served as canon to two presiding bishops of The Episcopal Church, as well as a longtime visiting professor at various seminaries and universities. Author or editor of many books, journals, and articles, as well as a film producer, Robertson holds several honorary degrees, including one from his alma mater, Virginia Theological Seminary.

The Rt. Rev. V. Gene Robinson was elected bishop of the Episcopal Diocese of New Hampshire on June 7, 2003, becoming the first openly gay and partnered bishop in historic Christianity. Despite national and international efforts to derail his ordination, he was consecrated a bishop on All Saints Sunday, November 2, 2003. After a decade serving as bishop of New Hampshire, Robinson worked as a senior fellow at the Center for American Progress, a progressive think tank in Washington, DC. Most recently, he served as vice president of religion and senior pastor at Chautauqua Institution in western New York. Since his retirement, he serves as a part of the worship team at the Washington National Cathedral. He has been honored by most civil rights/LGBTQ+ organizations for his advocacy on behalf of LGBTQ+ and other marginalized people. Bishop Robinson was invited by President-elect Barack Obama to give the invocation at the opening inaugural ceremonies at the Lincoln Memorial on January 18, 2009. He is the author of two books: *In the Eye of the Storm: Swept to the Center by God* (Seabury, 2008) and *God Believes in Love: Straight Talk about Gay Marriage* (Knopf, 2012) contributing to the national debate about marriage equality. He has been the subject of two feature-length documentaries: *For the Bible Tells Me So*, premiering at the 2006 Sundance Film Festival, and *Love Free or Die*, also premiering at Sundance, in 2012, winning the Special Jury Prize. Bishop Robinson is the proud father of two daughters and two granddaughters, and lives with his adorable dachshund boxer in Washington, DC.

The Rt. Rev. Samuel Rodman was ordained and consecrated as the XII Bishop of the Episcopal Diocese of North Carolina in Duke Chapel in 2017. Prior to his election, he served as the special projects officer for the Episcopal Diocese of Massachusetts where he engaged congregations, clergy and laity, in collaborative local and global mission. Prior to that, he spent sixteen years as the rector of St. Michael's in Milton, Massachusetts. Bishop Rodman is a graduate of Bates College and Virginia Theological Seminary. He and his wife of thirty-two years, Deborah, live in Raleigh. They are the parents of two adult daughters.

The Rt. Rev. Katharine Jefferts Schori served as bishop of Nevada, and then as presiding bishop of The Episcopal Church (2006–2015). She has taught in universities and seminaries, served as Assisting Bishop in San Diego, and occasionally assists in Los Angeles. She holds a PhD in oceanography and several honorary doctorates and continues to advocate for the health of the planet as a matter of justice for all creation.

Diana Turner-Forte is a dancer, healing arts practitioner, and writer. Her blog *Wonderfully Human* focuses on the intersection between spirit, the human form, and nature. She conducts private and small group classes that enable participants to explore the synergetic wholeness of body, mind, and soul through movement (dance), writing, and the healing power of the hands. Ms. Turner-Forte's essays have been published in *Stance on Dance*, *Universal Life* magazine, *Kosmos Journal*, and other periodicals. She's professed in the Third Order Society of St. Francis (TSSF) and resides in North Carolina.

Foreword

THE GREAT NEW ENGLAND Puritan divine Jonathan Edwards once likened true religion to the sweet taste of honey. In the *Treatise on Religious Affection*, Edwards asks us to imagine two individuals, one with no ability to taste food and the other with full use of the sense of taste. Both people admire honey; both see the warm golden color; both delight in the fragrance of honey just pulled from the comb. The individual without a sense of taste knows the properties of honey: she knows that it is sweet to the taste, she knows the gelid nature of its body, and its composition and manufacture by the extraordinary working of the honey bee. But she cannot know what the individual with the ability to taste can know directly, without description or analogy: the taste of honey.[1] This, Edwards tells us, is the difference between believers who have been given the gift of genuine Christian experience—a new principle of nature and of action—and those who can only imagine or view it from the outside. Religious awakening, Edwards says, is something like the venerable Carmelite doctrine of the spiritual senses: not an entirely new organ or sensibility but rather a new maxim and dynamism, an inner revolution within the old frame.

1. *A Treatise on Religious Affections*, part III.

Those who have been given this radical principle from Above know something indescribable, untranslatable into other words; they can taste the "Divine excellence."

A striking feature of the human sense organ is that the experience it renders is unique, immediate, and ineffable; it cannot be wholly captured in any third-party description. Honey, though fully capable of being analyzed in molecular terms, catalogued in chemical properties, and sorted into families of food or animal production, cannot be tasted by anyone for someone else. To the question "What does honey taste like?" the answer can only be given: "Try some!" The irreplaceably individual character of the faculty of taste is likened, in Edwards's essay, to the remaking of the inner self by grace: no one can experience the infusion of God's Presence, the communication of Divine healing, for another. It must be one's own, and words can never convey the depth, the vividness, the singularity of the near Presence of God. Edwards's appeal to the spiritual senses and their new foundation in God's justifying grace, avoids any labored attempt to speak of "pre-linguistic experience" or communion in alien tongue. Rather, the same human nature, the same powers and properties, the same inner sense, is now remade, elevated, repurposed to the Divine workings, and the principle of one's life is "born from above."

Edwards had good reason to take care with his examples and taxonomy. The Great Awakening had burnt through the Puritan stronghold of Northampton, Massachusetts, while Edwards was minister of the Reformed congregation there; he is widely considered the theologian and preacher of the movement. Like any revolution, this one stirred controversy. Some sprang from the unmistakable democratic impulse of revivalism. Evangelicalism, as this broad movement is now called, spread beyond the "Connecticut River gods," the powerful ministers of the old Congregational Churches, and gave voice to the laity, women in particular, and all those, however unschooled, who had tasted the Divine favor. (Abolition and nineteenth-century feminism evolved from this popular pietism.) Another objection to the Awakening was the haunting problem of inauthenticity. Any experience that is built upon the singular and unique, as is taste itself, falls pray to relativism and counterfeit. Familiar to many observers of religious revivals, in the eighteenth century and the present day, is the phenomenon of backsliding: many awakened believers in New England underwent periods of heightened fervor and devotion, only to find their hearts and imaginations cooling after a time, and religion losing its hold upon their lives. Such falling away made religious revival suspect to many Puritan divines—only a false clothing of religion could be found there, they said—and the Great Awakening was likened to the fire of apocalyptic visionaries at the close of the Middle Ages or to the fervor of the radical wing of the European Reformation, "enthusiasts," all. Soon congregations and theologians split over the awakened piety of the revival. New England Puritans divided over religious affections, the "Old Lights" from the "New." And Edwards himself would be driven from his pulpit in the aftermath of the Awakening and its lethargy soon after.

In the *Treatise on Religious Affection*, Edwards applied his considerable theological powers to questions that were hardly abstract for him. What could distinguish the hypocrite from the truly converted? How could one separate the effective calling of Christ from the external show of religion, similar in its outward signs and, for a time, its inner devotion, to the experience of true piety? The entire treatise is dedicated to answering these questions, ultimately appealing to the Augustinian discrimen of love as the truest, most lasting expression of religious life. Along the way, Edwards offers the example of taste as the beginning of proper insight into genuine Christian life.

This collection of essays, many deeply personal, and all richly disclosive of living and vital Christian faith, belongs securely in the field demarcated by Edwards's Treatise. In our contemporary idiom, we would refer to "religious experience" rather than "affection" and "belief" over "piety" or "effective calling," but the terrain is recognizably the same. The authors of these essays know the taste of honey, and the inexpressible inner renovation that God's Presence injects into their lives. Their testimonies here give us glimpses of what the taste of Divine things must be like, and how lives are uprooted, reordered, and set on the narrow path after experiencing inwardly, directly, and permanently the love of God in Christ Jesus. As the editors to this fine collection note in their preface, Episcopalians do not often use the language of piety and inner revival; much of church identity and history has been decidedly "Old Light." But the central axioms of Edwards's essay stand quietly in the background of many of these moving witnesses to Christ's effective call. The editors, too, are right to note the cost such Old Light predilections exact on the Episcopal Church. Not easily given to testifying to their conversion, or their prayer life, Episcopalians have been viewed culturally as mainline Establishment Protestants who do not allow embarrassing religious enthusiasms to cloud their carefully sanitized high-mindedness. These essays wonderfully subvert this caricature. These are red-blood narratives of Christian conversion, and the experience of prayer, of Divine guidance, and of mystical union is everywhere shouted abroad; nothing hidden here that will not be brought into the light. Little wonder that women and especially African American and Latina women speak powerfully here. Some inhabit cultural worlds where spiritual experience is readily understood and prized; and others recognize the revolutionary liberty that life in the Spirit affords. All the essays in this volume acknowledge the vast diversity of spiritual renewal and the manifold path it will take through liturgy, prayer, social action, and inner devotion.

These essays strike the reader forcibly by their immediacy and individuality. Nothing of bland spirituality about these chapters! They are particular and each in their own way incommunicable. Each of the authors strives to express the ineffable; each record that they tasted the Divine Excellence, and that words fail them. We cannot directly taste their experience—this after all is what immediacy amounts to. But we are allowed to hear how someone who has been reborn, and given a new principle of action, will tell that story, and we, the readers, can receive the echo of that transformation, and its searing power. Each repeat in their own idiom the fundamental axiom of Edwards's treatise, that religious awakening, like taste, is *original*; it cannot be described but only recognized. In this way, Bertrand Russell's celebration distinction between "knowledge by description" and "knowledge by acquaintance" is given contemporary dress. These essays do not argue or defend or explain; rather they simply report they have been encountered by Another, and they acknowledge it. They are summoned by this God, they see a new Truth, they know by intellection, not by discursive reason, and this experience is unshakable, primal. In reading these essay we too are invited: try it! Taste and see that the Lord is good. I cannot hope to summarize or do justice to the richness of these essays in the sketches below, but I will attempt to reflect some of the golden light that emerges there.

The democratic spirit of this New Light is manifest in many of these testimonies. Alta Gracia Perez Bullard writes of the liberative grace of God, the radical emancipation that awaits the Presence of God to the believer. Not always can she—or anyone else—live in the freedom God bestows directly on the believer's life; always the Christian is also the worldling, and the changes and chances of this life weigh heavy on all. But the recourse to prayer, to the Altar, to the inner Stillness who is God renews that spiritual and radical truth of her life, against all defilement and oppression. All nature speaks this silent, eternal word to her. Henry Atkins records a life given over, at great risk, to the egalitarian impulse of the Reign of God, drawing him into the Civil Rights Movement, into advocacy and defense of refugee camps in the midst of civil war and finally into environmental justice, the ecumenical ministry of his retirement years. The taste of Divine Nearness may be strictly individual and in the end incommunicable, yet it is hardly individualistic or solipsistic. It drives the believer, animated by a new principle, into the world, God's field, and makes them fearless, for "perfect love," John tells us, "casts out fear." Just so, the transforming and radical power of the Spirit called Tim Patterson into a ministry shaped by the "twin fires" of contemplation and prophecy, leading him into centering prayer, anti-poverty work, and AIDS advocacy. Sam Rodman depicts the abundance of the God who rains down manna upon the hungry, stirring up a congregation to prayer, to trust, and to daring commitment to the poor, the war-torn, the desperate. This is his "evangelical moment" where always there is more: more Eucharist, more confirmands, more funds, more confidence and hope. Lydia Bucklin experienced that abundance as a religious conversion, undergone not now as the minister but as the one ministered to, a rare experience that opened her eyes to the priesthood of strangers in their compassion and generosity to a woman suddenly uncertain where her next meal, and the meal of her child, would come from. The emancipatory Reign of God breaks in when the people of God both give and receive, each needy and each rich beyond telling, each knit up in the other, not now as strangers but as neighbors, as friends.

Charles Robertson conveys powerfully Edwards's conviction that the old forms of one's life are suffused with a new dynamism and direction, remade by a new principle of action. He was summoned by Christ, and his taste of the love of the Redeemer seized hold of his life and he could hardly find enough to read, enough to exegete, enough to discover of the Christian faith and its Holy Scriptures. Katharine Jefferts Schori found the summons to Christian discipleship always surprising, always unexpected, meeting her when other more recognizable, familiar, and expected vocational paths were closed; she was strengthened, authorized, sealed with an ambassadorship to the world. Gene Robinson encountered the crucified Lord who summoned, commissioned, and accepted him with love, and this new principle who is Divine Love freed and commandeered his life, in service to the church and to the world. Rayford Ray received this Love who is God, poured into his heart, by a fellow priest who spoke the word of love out of the depth of her suffering, her dementia, and her dying breath. Nothing else matters when the Love of God is the Anima of one's life.

Barney Hawkins, Ian Markham, and Linda Beatrice Brown, too, follow the Edwardian insight that a new principle laid in the foundation of one's nature reorients one's everyday life. The sting of grief began the search for God with urgency for Markham. Raised in a pietist household, Markham knew well the resources of the Christian life but the wrenching loss of his mother while he was still young sent him first into the far country, a land utterly distant from God, and then in due season to a fresh, immediate, and unmistakable knowledge of God at the very root of his life. A new principle was forged in the old pathways of faith and discipleship. Life is now suffused by a warmth and peace the world cannot give, and the neighbor is bound up in Markham's life just because his life is bound up with God's. Barney Hawkins movingly depicts the way in which his daughter, Ellen, has become the living principle of God's Presence to him: her generosity and readiness to forgive; her courage and attention to others; her warmth and style and exuberance; all signs of God's utter abundant self-giving in his life and in the life of all who call upon him. Linda Beatrice Brown found the Lord's eyes trained upon her as a young child, affirming her unique call through the entrancing beauty of a crabapple in spring bloom. This became the principle of her life, carrying her through illness, through seasons of dryness, and now, in the grace-filled experience of poetry, a deepening of prayer and of spiritual wisdom, through Mary, the Mother of God.

Finally, we read of lives transformed by spiritual senses heightened through the immediate experience of God. The sense of hearing, most especially of music, resonates throughout this collection. Santana Alvarado anchors his religious experience in hymnody, "Jesus Loves Me" as earliest example. Psalms, camp songs, pop songs recast as devotional prayers, compositions for Alvardo's family in Puerto Rico: all speak of a Christian life animated by the God who "hears the rights of the destitute, and defends the rights of the poor and needy." Brooks Graebner recounts a life touched from earliest days by music, especially the keyboard arts; he was drawn into the church by the invitation to take his pianism into the sanctuary, accompanying the liturgy by organ. At the end of his working career, he writes movingly of returning to the complex world of the organ, and discovering the mystery who is God in the Bach French-style fantasia, *Pièce D'orgue*. God has time for us, Barth wrote, and exhibits this Divine patience in waiting for us to come to know and to love Him. Bach's stunning architectonic in this masterwork for the organ intimates that Divine patience, and Graebner testifies to his sense of wonder, of waiting, and of contemplation as he labors to master this virtuoso work of the organ repertory. Kimberly Dunn is a musician who brings her knowledge and love of movement and of harmony directly into her religious experience of Divine intimacy. Hers is a testimony to the medieval tradition of the spiritual marriage between Christ and the believer, and it is refreshingly and unhesitatingly embodied, sensual, and fearless. A new principle of devotion, loyalty, and joy now animate Dunn's life and her experience must speak to anyone who knows, directly and truly, that God is love.

Kim Coleman found the elixir of dance and of song to testify to her experience of God's healing Presence, delivering her sister from chronic pain, and accompanying her own life with direction, with confidence and with joy. The celebrated Fannie Crosby hymn, "I Come to the Garden Alone," has become the spiritual sense of hearing for Coleman. Dance has expressed the religious experience of other essayists. Diana Turner-Forte combines her own professional life in a classical dance corps with her liturgical dance, a direct enactment of her childhood conviction that the Holy Spirit indwelt her own body.

These rich and revealing memoirs of the spiritual life will give the reader a taste of the conversion that awaits all who seek the God who has sought and called them. Jonathan Edwards described a religious world that exceeded all description, an immediacy and a delight that could only be tasted afresh from the Divine grace. May the Good God bestow on all who happen upon these testimonies a taste of this Infinite Love: nothing will remain the same afterward but behold, all will become new.

Katherine Sonderegger

Preface

THE EDITORS

EPISCOPALIANS ARE FAMOUS FOR their liturgy, music, and their thoughtful approach to faith and prayer. However, we are less famous for our willingness to talk about our faith and, in particular, our experience of God. In this book, we are inviting distinguished Episcopalians to reflect on their experience of God. When did they sense the presence of God? How did they experience the presence of God? What is prayer like? How do they pray? What is it like to walk each day with Jesus? How seriously do we take the promptings of the Holy Spirit? How does the "transcendent" feel in their lives? How does the "transcendent" show up in their daily lives?

The book is divided into sections. The first section captures moments of divine engagement with an individual in a direct way. In the literature, this would be seen as a direct religious experience, of the like that the mystics entertained. In the second section, we have more indirect religious experiences—experiences mediated through people or places or the liturgy. We do appreciate that this is in many ways a contrived distinction—after all, all feelings are mediated in some way. In addition, we are very aware that certain chapters are actually both; so the editors attempted to make the difficult decision to locate the chapter on the basis of the balance of the chapter.

We hope this will be a book that can be read and studied by Episcopalians. It is a book intended to help a Christian reflect on their own experience of the divine. Our hope is for the Christian to be liberated from personal shame or an awkwardness provoked by the reactions of others. This is a space of exploration, discovery, transformation, and evolution to make known the true self and the reality of God.

We believe the implications of our failure to talk more intimately about our faith are significant. Too many skeptics about faith focus exclusively on the "beliefs" and do not appreciate the "experience" dimension. As the Rev. Dr. Kate Sonderegger notes knowing about honey is not the same as tasting honey. There is some evidence that our inability to talk more intimately about our faith has meant that our tradition is largely confined to a certain demographic (elderly, college educated); and it is possible that these and other demographics want to hear or know what it is like to "sense God" and walk "closely to Jesus" or what it means to "walk in the Spirit." As our world evolves so must our faith and with this book, the intention is to demonstrate that this "mystical" and "experiential" strand is indeed in the Episcopal Church. This book is an invitation for us all to talk rather more about our sense of God.

Acknowledgments

From Kimberly Dunn and Ian Markham

The editors are grateful to the commissioning editor—Robin Parry—and for the remarkable team at Cascade—George Callihan, and copy editor Stephanie Hough. We are grateful to Paul Flynn, who helped with the final stages of the book.

We are both very grateful for the willingness of Dr. Katherine Sonderegger to write the foreword. The gift of her reflections is much appreciated.

We were delighted and touched that our contributors were so positive in their response; in the end, the quality of their personal stories is exceptionally high and very moving. Thank you for sharing your soul with us all.

From Kimberly Dunn

The spiritual and theological experiences from my childhood to present day have contributed to the formation of my life journey. I had not thought of making those experiences public until Dr. Kate Sonderegger created space for me to verbally share an experience of God. I am grateful for her attunement to the Spirit of God. Her encouragement gave me permission to write it down. I pray I will never forget that day in Dr. Kate's office where I was liberated.

I am grateful to The Very Rev. Dr. Ian Markham, for seeing the value of such a topic to share with the Episcopal Church and the world. I am especially grateful for his willingness and support to come alongside me in this spiritual literary endeavor. I appreciate his company—he is a gift.

It is with gratitude I recognize my professors at Virginia Theological Seminary for acknowledging my humanity and theological expression without judgement—Shawn Strout, Sharon Heaney, Judy Fentress-Willimans, John Yueh Han Yeah, Joseph Thompson, Altagracia Perez-Bullard, Lisa Kimball, Robert Heaney, Stephen Cook, Ruthanna Hooke, Marty Wheeler, Elizabeth DeGaynor, and Mark Jefferson.

Moving and selling the place we called home for over sixteen years to go to seminary was an emotional decision made possible by the support of my sons, Kendall Dunn and Noah Dunn. Their love is priceless. I also acknowledge the unconditional loyalty of my dog, Lucie, who is continually by my side or on my lap to remind me that love is always present.

From Ian Markham

The idea of this book was a gift. I am grateful to my co-editor, who was inspired to suggest this book. Her chapter started as a paper in a course taught by Dr. Kate Sonderegger and me. She offered up her "experience of God." It was profound, moving, and insightful. Having planted the idea, the journey of this book began.

Writing is my joy. The Board of Trustees encourages my writing; and I am especially grateful to David Charlton, the board chair. I am grateful to the senior team who tolerate these seasons when a book project is my priority—Melody Knowles, Jacqui Ballou, Linda Dienno, Lisa Kimball, Nicky Burridge, Rachelle Sam, and Michael DeLashmutt. My work life is held together by the talented and gifted Taryn Habberley.

ACKNOWLEDGMENTS

Working on a project of this nature comes from one's heart. And those closest to my heart are my wife, Lesley Markham, and our son, Luke, and his fiancée, Sam Brooks. Maddie the dog came and sat next to me as I finished editing the book; for her companionship, I am grateful.

—— SECTION ONE ——

Living Aware of God

1

Dance with Me

A Mystical Experience
with My Beloved

BY KIMBERLY E. DUNN

E'en like two little bank-dividing brooks,
That wash the pebbles with their wanton streams,
And having rang'd and search'd a thousand nooks,
Meet both at length in silver-breasted Thames,
Where in a greater current they conjoin:
So I my best-beloveds am; so he is mine.

E'en so we met; and after long pursuit,
E'en so we join'd; we both became entire;
No need for either to renew a suit,
For I was flax and he was flames of fire:
Our firm united souls did more then twine;
So I my best-beloveds am; so he is mine.

. . .

Nor Time, nor Place, nor Chance, nor Death can bow
My least desires unto the least remove;

He's firmly mine by oath; I his by vow;
He's mine by faith; and I am his by love;
He's mine by water; I am his by wine;
Thus I my best-beloveds am; thus he is mine.

He is my Altar; I, his Holy Place;
I am his guest; and he, my living food;
I'm his by penitence; he mine by grace;
I'm his by purchase; he is mine, by blood;
He's my supporting elm; and I his vine:
Thus I my best-beloveds am; thus he is mine.

He gives me wealth, I give him all my vows:
I give him songs; he gives me length of days:
With wreaths of grace he crowns my conquering brows:
And I his Temples with a crown of Praise,
Which he accepts as an everlasting sign,
That I my best-beloveds am; that he is mine.[1]

I OPEN THIS ARTICLE with this poem by Francis Quarels because I identify with both its poetic and spiritual qualities and message. It also depicts several images that can be identified in both secular and non-secular world views around love, union, surrender, and belonging and what may be obvious to me may not be to others. Upon reading the poem, I immediately thought of my relation and communion with my Best-Beloved, God. I will now ask you, the reader, to journey with me on the path of definition, personal experience, insight and perspective of Christian mysticism. Notice, I do not ask that you agree or disagree but to simply journey. I pray I do it justice, bring glory to my Best-Beloved, and open a space for you, the reader, to imagine possibilities. I hope my account creates a pathway for others toward a soul and spiritual liberation out of

1. Francis Quarels, *Quarles' Emblems (1886)*. https://publicdomainreview. org/collection/quarles-emblems-1886..

shame and/or suppression. God desires people to live abundant, wholesome lives free from guilt and oppression. This is also my prayer and heart's compassion for you, the reader, to experience or to simply make peace with an experience of God you have hidden and dared not to acknowledge as truth.

I am now upon the time in which I am to share one of the most sacred, intimate, mystical and holy experiences of my existence in this life. This does not come with ease to share with the world but comes with the permeation of truth, of all that is true, beautiful, timeless, and holy through the witness of my soul. A close friend of mine once said to me on my mystical journey, "Ego is of the mind. Self is of the Soul. Let your Soul be a witness." In his book called *Mysticism: A Study and An Anthology*, F. C. Happold who was an educational pioneer and dared to place mysticism in the modern world asserts the following:

The nature of man is not a single but a dual one. He has not one but two selves, the phenomenal *ego*, of which he is chiefly conscious and which he tends to regard as his true self, and a non-phenomenal, eternal self, an inner man, the spirit, the spark of divinity within him, which is his true self. It is possible for a man, if he so desires and is prepared to make the necessary effort, to identify himself with his true self and so with the Divine Ground, which is of the same or like nature.[2]

So, here I am. In the presence of the I AM, presenting the full portion of one of several personal records of my encounters with God. Since I have experienced God in various ways, I desired the next layer and put forth the necessary effort to identify myself with my true self. My soul has been and *is* a witness of God's presence. I have not walked or spoken in the fullness of the mystical part of who I am because there has been and are currently debates on mystical experiences on whether they are true and are given to people by God. Some skeptics say that the mind is playing tricks because it may have been altered by substances that produce delusions or hallucinations. Some believe that mystical experiences are

2. F. Crossfield Happold, *Mysticism: A Study and an Anthology* (Baltimore: Penguin, 1963), 20.

imaginations on overload of those who desire to draw attention to themselves. Those reasons no longer bind me for now I give an account of my mystical self.

To have a better understanding of mystical experiences is to have a foundational understanding of mysticism. Mysticism has been around for centuries and has contributed greatly to the Christian faith tradition through great philosophers, theologians, and Bible scholars. Mysticism is the sense of some form of contact with the Divine or transcendent. In the Christian tradition it can involve union with God, in which a person may experience another space that is not the conscious reality of the ego. It is a deep spiritual connection beyond knowing. To experience this way of being, a person must allow themselves to let go of ego—their identity—and just "be."

I began having mystical experiences and dreams when I was a child. Along with how I saw Christianity and personal relationships with God lived out through my mother and grandmother, my understanding of the meaning of God shifted and changed over many years. I began to *see* God differently. I saw God as Creator and the One who wants to save us through His Son, Jesus. I saw God as my Daddy because I was raised by my mother and grandmother. As I got older, I began to see God as Pursuer to become the Lover of my Soul. I saw God as The Promise Keeper, Protector, Sustainer, Provider, and Vindicator. I saw God as Male, Female, and then Who or What God needed to be to me at times in desperate need and in those times of joy unspeakable. Now, I see God as Transcendent Love. Katherine Sonderegger sums up the Perfection of the Divine Love like this:

> Love is the keystone of the Divine Perfection, we should say, the Attribute that holds together, sums up, and makes lovely the entire Divine Nature, all its Properties and its Glory. —It is the Perfection of Eternity in its loveliest Form. God's Love is the greatest of all that lasts; it is the excellent Way.[3]

3. Katherine Sonderegger, *Systematic Theology*. Vol. 1, *The Doctrine of God* (Minneapolis: Fortress, 2015), 469.

Francis Quarels's poem in which I began my essay along with Sonderegger's summary of Love gives me permission to *be* and *act* out love with Love in full abandon. As I have digressed for a moment, I would like to continue to share about my mystical experiences and what happens. In those sometimes-spontaneous moments, I have observed that my ego dissolved to where I had no recollection of its essence. In this particular account which I will share, I was aware of myself being escorted into a total rapture of a holy presence beyond my consciousness in which my body was passionately responding. In the beginning, my ego was aware of what was happening; however, I was unsure and felt apprehension of the unknown—but I was curious. My curiosity got the best of me and thus, I let go. I surrendered. I surrendered my ego. I surrendered control in exchange for the curious in which I felt unusually safe. I write this essay because I believe the time has come for me to share this experience and out of an act of obedience from the leading of the Holy Spirit.

My mystical experience came at a time in my life in which I had been spending numerous hours with God. There was nothing in particular that made me want to make spiritual space at this point and time in my life, just a desire to do so. I read and meditated on Scriptures and sat quietly in contemplation almost daily. I was a thirty-three-year-old wife and mother of one child. It seemed that every moment I had free, I used it to converse with God. Spiritually, this way of being drew me closer and closer in communion with the Lover of my Soul. As days passed, I started feeling a continual presence of the Holy Spirit throughout my day. Each morning, I began to look forward to making time and spending time with God as like that of a lover and her Beloved. I was looking for time to "steal away" like that of a young girl who is curious and delighted at the fact that she is being pursued by her Beloved. The excitement, for me, was in the arranging of daily life to create a space of time to read Scripture, pray, and meditate on what Paul suggests we should rest our thoughts on in Phil 4:8: "whatever is true, whatever is honorable, whatever is just, whatever is pure, whatever is pleasing, and whatever is commendable, if there is any excellence and if there is anything worthy of praise, think about these things" (NRSV).

Upon arrival of our spiritual times together, I came prepared in a state of openness and surrender to receive whatever God wanted to share with me. One particular day, I heard a voice that said, "Come be with Me." As I perceived it to be the voice of the Lord, I responded with saying that if this is You, God, please make a way for me to be with You. I had never left my family to be alone without them and I did not want my husband to become suspicious. Two days later, my spouse shared that he needed some time away to relax and refresh. I shared with him that I wanted to spend some time in prayer with God. He and I had a conversation and agreed that each of us would take a weekend for ourselves. I was simply amazed how quickly God provided a way for me to spend time with Him. Romans 8:28 confirmed "that all things work together for the good of those who love God, who are called according to his purpose" (NRSV). At this point, I was full of amazement and could hardly wait to be with my Beloved.

Preparing for the weekend was very unusual for me and I felt a little peculiar not only having never gone anywhere without my spouse and child but also actively planning a rendezvous with God. Although it felt a little eccentric, I genuinely felt what I was doing was right. I felt the need to keep moving forward. I felt secure in all of my thoughts and actions leading up to meeting with God. I had no idea what would transpire but was fully open to receive all that God wanted to share with me. As my weekend approached, I asked the Spirit to show me what I needed to pack. This is when things got a little strange and surprising. I was moved by the Spirit to pack the sheer, white negligee hanging in my closet. It was a gift from my bridal shower that I had never worn. At that moment, I felt the need to attend to the waves of past thoughts and actions that led me to this very moment. As each moment came back to me, I embraced each step as though gathering puzzle pieces to connect them together to see the picture. It began to make sense to me. This moment became real for me. God beckoned me, made a way for me to meet Him, and chose for me to wear the sheer, white negligee that was a bridal shower gift that had not been worn. After being married eleven years, it seemed like the sheer, white negligee was kept and meant just for this time with Him. Although unusual and strange, I knew I was following the Spirit. I felt no shame. Instead, I felt thrills of anticipation. I felt pleasantly aroused and energetic like I was going to meet my Lover—and I was. I wondered, what was God up to? I made up in my mind that I would never tell anyone about this because they would not believe me or understand.

It was Friday, and off I was for my weekend with God. I packed my Bible, CD player for meditation music, notebooks, pens, devotionals, a recording device, a few clothing items, and the sheer, white negligee. I stayed in prayer and quiet as I drove to the local motel. I told God that I would fully trust all of my steps and destinations during our time together because I knew he would not lead me astray and he would protect me. I was in full surrender mode. Once settled in my motel room, I prayed and knew to wait in silence. Not the silence of which the ego gives way to perpetuate a sense of control of consciousness but the silence that "is the nothingness of the beyond"[4] that Dr. Llewellyn Vaughan-Lee, a Sufi teacher, writes about in his book, *The Bond with the Beloved*. "It is in this space," he continues, "that we remain inwardly attentive to the Beloved, always receptive to His hint."[5]

God's presence was familiar to me, and I knew I was not alone. Our weekend had begun, and I was moved to go to dinner. I arrived at the restaurant and was seated at a table for two. This was perfect. This was the first time I had gone to dinner "alone" but I wasn't alone. My ego became an antagonist with my soul because I was now in a space with people. I was functioning on the inner and outer planes simultaneously. My ego reminded me that this was unnatural and tried to make me feel unstable and off-centered. I remembered with Whom I was having dinner and the needle

4. Llewellyn Vaughn-Lee, *The Bond with The Beloved* (Point Reyes, CA: The Golden Sufi Center, 2012), 109.

5. Vaughn-Lee, *The Bond with the Beloved*, 109.

re-centered. After dinner, I returned to the motel in quiet. I prayed and waited. I fell into a deep and wholesome sleep.

Saturday morning, I awakened still in the presence of the Lord. I said my morning prayers aloud and acknowledged God's presence with thanksgiving. Things began to shift. The feeling of God's presence became more intense. All of my senses were heightened. I could feel my heartbeat. My body started feeling sensations of anticipation. Without words or questions, I was moved to put on the sheer, white negligee. All the sensations in my body intensified and I felt God's presence within and without. The room began to pale in recognition as though to depict another space. Once I was fully dressed in the sheer, white negligee without undergarments, I stopped, waited and listened. I began to faintly hear music. The music became more distinct. It was not like any music I had heard before. It was beyond beautiful and then . . . I heard these words, "Dance with Me."

There, in my sheer, white negligee, I danced like I had never danced before. I felt the presence of God in every ounce of the room. I smelled a sweet fragrance that was unrecognizable to my senses but somehow familiar. The music was clear, pleasant, and moving as to guide my steps. I felt the fragrance and music to be intentional in their apprehension of the space, time, and of me. I felt so much joy and pleasure. I was overwhelmed with peace. I felt secure. I felt an all-encompassing unity with my Lover and his Love. That is What and Who was in the room. Love. I no longer saw the room, I did not care about the room. The space had been altered. I had been altered. My being had been altered. I was unconscious to time. It felt like someone was holding me in their arms and dancing with me. I had no cares. It was just me and the Lover of my soul intertwined, genuine, complete, earthy, whole, and holy. I began to cry gentile tears that were a result of the passion I felt through every inch of my body and soul and every inch of the space. I could not speak, nor did I desire to speak. Goose pimples manifested as a result of the existential feelings upon my body as if to have been gently caressed. I was with my God. I was my Beloved's and he was mine. A union of magnificence. I felt a transcendence, unexplainable and full of the glory of God. I did not care where I was because I was with him and . . . I was safe. We danced.

Lost in an intentional timeless space, the music and sweet fragrance began to leisurely fade. I began to slowly come out of this state of trance. I began to recognize where I was and what I was doing. I began to remember the sheer, white negligee. I fought to not "come back" to my present reality of matter and substance. I wanted to stay in that realm of sweetness and safety. The music and sweet fragrance faded until they were no more. The steps to the dance slowed to a pause. I stopped and listened. I took a long deep breath and let it out gradually as my body relaxed. I fell upon the bed exhausted but feeling alive and well. I fell asleep. I awakened and it was dusk. I had nothing to eat or drink. I was famished. After eating, in silence and stillness, I pondered what had happened. I was pleased and I believe I pleased God. Later, in the night, I wondered why me, Lord? I got an intuition, why not me?

Sunday morning, about an hour before check out, God began to speak to me about things that had not yet come concerning my immediate family. God also encouraged me to continue to be who I am which is who he made me to "be." I will pause here for now so to move on and share with you, the reader, my insight and perspective of prayer and spending time with God. Once again, as the reader, I ask that you simply journey with me. If you are still reading, I thank you for sharing this special experience that has contributed to my spiritual formation as a woman who is black, Christian, and in love with the Beloved. I continue to have mystical experiences and I believe the account I shared, along with others, is the will of God and the possible result of what can happen when a person gives themselves totally over to prayer. My insight and perspective culminates with the outcome of prayer. When a person prays and surrenders, the Omnipotence of God is clear. Saint Teresa of Avila on her conviction of prayer which can be found in *The Book of Her Life: The Autobiography of St. Teresa of Avila* states:

1. Enough has been said of this manner of prayer, and of what the soul has to do, or rather, to speak more correctly, of what God is doing within it; for it is he who now takes upon himself the gardeners' work, and who will have the soul take its ease; except that the will is consenting to the graces, the fruition of which it has, and that it must resign itself to all that the True Wisdom would accomplish in it— . . .

2. My meaning is that, in a state of prayer, so high as this, the soul understands that God is doing his work without any fatiguing of the understanding, except that, as it seems to me, it is as if amazed in beholding our Lord taking upon himself the work of the good gardener, refusing to let the soul undergo any labor whatever, but that of taking its pleasure in the flowers beginning to send forth their fragrance; for when God raises a soul up to this state, it can do all this, and much more,—for these are the effects of it.[6]

Prayer: Open the eyes of our hearts, Lord,
so that we may see You. Amen.

Reflection, Contemplation, and Discussion Questions

1. Did the author's experience make you feel uncomfortable or were you able to identify with the experience in a particular way?

2. What might be some helpful insights that can be applied to your own spiritual growth and relationship with God from this experience?

6. Teresa of Avila, *St. Teresa of Avila Three Book Treasury—Interior Castle, The Way of Perfection, and The Book of Her Life (Autobiography).* Translated by E. Allison Peers and Benedictines of Stanbrook. Illustrated Edition (Aurora, CO: Chump Change, 1921), 261.

3. Ps 46:10 states, "He says, 'Be still, and know that I am God.'" When have you felt a need to stop and pray or to stop and listen?

2

Beyond Your Wildest Imagining

BY BISHOP GENE ROBINSON

They lock up people who claim to have
visions from God.

I WAS A FIRST-YEAR seminarian, and a recent confirmand in the
Episcopal Church. Dean Sam Wiley took a small group of semi-
narians each week to a different location in New York City to talk
with ordinary Christians doing extraordinary ministry in God's
Name. That week, we went to visit two monks of the Italian mo-
nastic order Little Brothers of Jesus, living and ministering in the
crime-and-drugs-rampant Lower East Side.

I was moved and challenged by the simplicity and holiness
of these two men and their lives of service to the poor and marginalized. From the time we arrived and throughout the Eucharist we shared in their tiny "chapel," I kept thinking, "What am I
doing here?" and "Who do I think I am to be here, beginning a
journey toward priesthood?! I've got a big ego and a big mouth,
not the humility immediately obvious in these monks. And besides, I'm scared to death of confirming my worst fears: I'm gay
and God is disgusted by me, and I am unfit for ordination." By

the end of the communion service, I was ready to leave this holy outpost and leave seminary itself. I stayed behind in this little rustic chapel to pray, while my classmates helped the brothers prepare spaghetti in the kitchen. And then it happened.

I don't know how else to say it: Jesus appeared to me. He was still alive, hanging on the cross. I could see down to about his knees, he was labored in his breathing. He didn't say anything, nor did I. But I was overwhelmed by Love. In the silence I heard/felt/ saw God loving me as I was. More viscerally than ever before, I knew that God loved me "beyond my wildest imagining." It filled me with gratitude and humility. The answer to my question "Who do I think I am?!" came in the silence and in the presence of the living Christ hanging on the cross: "I love you, I called you, and I will make you fit for ministry in my Name."

I don't know how long I was there. It may have been seconds or minutes or longer. The vision dissipated. And immediately I began to doubt, looking for cracks in the walls that might suggest the shape of a cross. When I emerged from the chapel to join the others, I was fearful that my face would be obviously shining and bright. After all, wasn't that what happened to Moses when he talked with God? It was such a private and inexplicable experience, I didn't speak of it to anyone for twenty or so years, and then only to a very few.

Some thirty years later, I was ordained, out as a gay man with a partner, nominated for bishop in my home diocese, and gathered with others at the diocesan bishop election held on June 7, 2003, at St. Paul's Church, Concord, New Hampshire. After the first ballot, it was clear I was going to be the people's choice to become their next bishop, making me the first openly gay and partnered priest to be made bishop in historic Christianity. And although I can't prove it, at the very moment my election was announced and the congregation erupted into a roar of surprise and joy, a "wind" blew through the inside of St. Paul's Church—the kind of thing, according to Scripture, that happens when the Holy Spirit is at work doing something. I can't explain it, but it was experienced and spoken of by many in attendance, some of whom described it as the most significant experience of God of their lifetimes. The Holy Spirit, it seemed, was doing something new. Before I even made it home that afternoon, I received my first death threat.

Death threats would become an almost-daily experience for me and would last for a couple of years. My partner Mark, who offered profound and sacrificial support throughout this journey, and I decided that we would not cover all our windows at home, to prevent being killed by a would-be assassin, because to do so would mean "they" would have won. No, we would simply keep trying to do the next right thing, trusting that whether or not it would result in my assassination, it was what God called me to. And however it might end, it would be okay. Or rather, God would make it okay, whatever that looked like or turned out to be.

I was supported (and loved) by the people of my diocese, by family and friends, and by my spouse. I was overwhelmed and humbled by the steadfastness of their love. But at the end of the day, it was simply me, walking through the valley of the shadow of death, praying that the Good Shepherd would restore my soul and "lead me in paths of righteousness for his name's sake."

I began to find my own experience in Scripture itself in ways I had never really noticed before, none better than Ps 27, which became my mantra, in which the psalmist complains to God about his enemies who are gathered around him, wanting to devour his flesh. That felt about right to me, as hatred and vitriol came unceasingly in my direction. And though I wasn't there yet, I could practice saying the words of the psalmist in hopes of believing them myself:

> The Lord is my light and my salvation;
> > whom shall I fear?
> The Lord is the stronghold of my life;
> > of whom shall I be afraid?
> Though an army encamp against me,
> my heart shall not fear;
> though war rise up against me,
> yet I will be confident.

This psalm gave me words to say, expressing my longing for trust in God, before and even when I didn't feel confident. And the psalmist's proclamation slowly became my own reoriented goal:

> One thing I asked of the Lord,
> that will I seek after:
> to live in the house of the Lord
> all the days of my life,
> to behold the beauty of the Lord,
> and to inquire in his temple.
> For he will hide me in his shelter
> in the day of trouble;
> he will conceal me under the cover of his tent;
> he will set me high on a rock.
> Now my head is lifted up
> above my enemies all around me,
> and I will offer in his tent
> sacrifices with shouts of joy;
> I will sing and make melody to the Lord.

I began to actually believe that I didn't need to be the perfect bishop (nor did God expect me to be). I didn't need to get everything right, nor say the perfect words in every interview, nor never be fearful, to be precious in the eyes of God. This wasn't about "winning" anything. The prize had already been won for me on the Cross and awarded to me simply because I am God's child, witnessing to what I know: that I am loved beyond my wildest imagining by the God of all that is. No qualifiers. No prerequisites. No exceptions listed in the fine print. Just love. And because of it, I could make a witness, my witness, to that love operating in my life. And whether I did that well or poorly, it wouldn't change God's love for me.

Miraculously, and importantly, it turns out that that is precisely what drove my enemies crazy. Cruel characterizations, withering judgment, and vicious attacks couldn't defeat me (though

often they would discourage and frighten me). When one is that
certain of God's love, there's no end to what one can bear.

So, how did I come to know God's love in that way? Sure,
I grew up with "Jesus loves me this I know," and "I am with you
always, even to the end of time." It was the change in my prayer
life that made me actually believe it.

When the challenges of being a good bishop for the people
of my diocese filled my days, and fears about what might happen
invaded my dreams at night, I turned to my spiritual director, The
Rev. Margaret Bullit-Jonas. Her pastoral care and wisdom saved my
spiritual life—partly because she taught me a new way to pray.

I remember her saying to me something like, "You know,
I think you talk too much in your prayers. God hardly gets any
air time. Let me suggest this: Get yourself in a prayerful posture
(physically and mentally), close your eyes, and invite God in. Then
sit there and shut up." (Given her kind and peaceful nature, I doubt
that she actually said "shut up"! But I got the message.) "Don't say
anything, don't do anything, don't try to accomplish anything, don't
plan anything, don't complain about anything, don't occupy your
mind with anything else, other than being open to God. And just sit
with it. And let God do what God does best: love you.

"Imagine," she instructed, "God's love as light or warmth,
starting at the top of your head, and oozing down over your
body like warm butter, drenching you in God's love, acceptance,
understanding, care, and genuine affection for you. Don't try to
do anything with it. Don't try to figure it out. Don't even worry
about 'is it working?!' Just let it be what it is. This is not going
to be about what you are doing, but about what God is doing
because of God's love for you."

It would be an understatement to say that this was anything
like how I had prayed up until this time. And as an off-the-scale
extrovert, telling me not to say anything was asking for a miracle.
At first, I just couldn't do it. I'd start imagining the light or warmth
of God, and before I knew it, my mind was making the grocery
list for later. "Don't worry," she told me. "Thoughts and concerns
will pass by you like a bus passing a street corner. And sometimes

(maybe even often, at first) you'll get on that bus and find yourself far from where you wanted to be. Just get off that 'bus' and return to God's warmth and light."

Even after I got somewhat used to this prayer practice, sometimes I just couldn't do it. Often, I'd feel like I hadn't "done it" right and was a failure. I'd find myself thinking, "How could something as simple as this give me what I need?!" But as this practice—which is really about allowing God to be an active player in my relationship with God—began to indeed, give me what I needed, I began to trust it. It was okay if I couldn't point to any successful "product" on a particular day. It was to be expected that sometimes my mind would wander, or that I'd become skeptical that I was "doing it right." What was important was faithfully returning to it, day after day after day, being assured that God was always present and waiting for me to be present.

And here's what I came to understand about myself and about God:

I'm not unlike a pre-kindergartner, unsure of myself and reluctant, even frightened, to leave my family and go out into the world. My ability to "go out" is directly proportional to my confidence that when I "come home," I will find understanding, empathy, and love. And when I have my confidence replenished by that kind of support from my parents, I'm ready to venture into the bigger world and to do bigger things.

Being a Christian, it seems to me, is a lot like that. Every day, out in the world, my self-esteem, and therefore my confidence, is eroded by every sort of force that seeks to diminish me. That empowering confidence needs replenishing on a daily, sometimes hourly, basis. God's love for me is what replenishes my ability to go out and be God's loving arms and witness in and to the world. But I have to stop long enough and offer myself fully enough for God to have that effect on me. Not to do so is a sure recipe for burnout, cynicism, and hopelessness.

In my life, I need my tank of confidence (which empowers me) to be refilled by the One who calls me out into the world. That prayer practice allowed me not only to survive, but to thrive in the decade I served the people of the Diocese of New Hampshire. I'd like to say that I still practice this way of praying on a daily basis. I don't. I don't doubt that I still need it; it's just that I don't need it as desperately and viscerally as I did during that dangerous decade in my life. But I know it saved my spiritual life at a time I needed it most. I'll be forever grateful to Margaret for teaching me to use it. And I will be eternally grateful to God who showed up, and continues to show up, whether I do or not.

Five years after retiring from my work in New Hampshire, 2018 marked the twentieth anniversary of the death of Matthew Shepard, the young gay college student brutally beaten and left for dead, hanging on a Wyoming prairie fence. It turns out that Matt's parents had never buried Matt's ashes, for fear that anti-gay protesters would desecrate his grave. I approached the Washington National Cathedral to see if they might be willing to receive and inter Matt's ashes. Their "yes" was offered without hesitation. Carrying Matt's ashes up the center aisle of that awesome church was one of the great privileges of my life. But what was more awe-inspiring was watching the four thousand or so people—mostly LGBTQ+—who were there, despite the church, synagogue, or mosque's being the scene of their greatest oppression and mistreatment. They wanted to know what I had wanted to know in the chapel of that small East Village apartment, the home of two humble monks, some fifty years ago: Does God love me? If a church can joyously welcome the ashes of Matthew Shepard, can it mean that they might love and welcome me too? Do I dare believe it? And what difference will it make?

My life has been spent with one foot in the church and one foot in the LGBTQ+ community, trying to explain each to the other, begging each to give the other a chance. On the day we buried Matt and interred his ashes at the National Cathedral, both of my worlds came together, for at least that moment. And I felt like God had been preparing me for that day my whole life.

I have a magnet on my refrigerator which reads: "God loves you. But I'm his favorite." The miracle is that each one of us is God's favorite and that God loves not only me beyond my imagining, but that God loves you just as much.

Reflection, Contemplation, and Discussion Questions

1. Do you believe God loves you unconditionally? Does the author's testimony offer you reassurance? How has your belief of God's unconditional love formed your faith?

2. The author shared, "When one is that certain of God's love, there is no end to what one can bear." Does this statement bring on anxiety or does it offer comfort or confidence? What thoughts come to mind when reading this statement?

3. How has the author's experience of God changed, supported, or shifted your thoughts and acceptance about the LGBTQA+ community? In what ways?

3

Saying Yes to a Slow Dance with God

By Kim Coleman

I come to the garden alone,
While the dew is still on the roses;
And the voice I hear, falling on my ear,
The Son of God discloses.
And He walks with me, and He talks with me,
And He tells me I am His own,
And the joy we share as we tarry there,
None other has ever known.[1]

IT IS WELL PAST my preteen bedtime of 9:00 p.m. when I find myself rolling out of bed and onto the carpeted floor that cushions
my landing. The room is dark. I can barely make out the outline of
the furniture that fills the space. A night table. A dresser. The other
twin bed where my younger sister is soundly sleeping. I move
quickly and I move quietly. The last thing I want is to awaken her
even though I need to pray.

---

1. C. Austin Miles, 1913, https://hymnary.org/text/i_come_to_the_garden
_alone.

We had spent most of the day, once again, visiting doctors to see if they can diagnose why my sister is having splitting headaches. Time and time again those doctors report finding no medical reason for her symptoms. Meanwhile she continues to suffer, especially during the night. It is an uncustomary grace to find her fast asleep.

As soon as my knees hit the floor, I begin to sob. Before long I add garbled words to my incessant flow of tears: *God, please help my sister. God, please take away her pain. God, Nana said if I ever needed help all I had to do was call on Jesus. I need help, God. Jesus, please help us.*

I don't remember the content of the promises I make along with my fervent petitions to God, but I am pretty sure I promise God everything. From *take my life* to *I'll do whatever you want me to do*, my pleas cover the gamut. Nor do I recall whether the tone I use with God is reverent and dignified or more likely reflective of the urgency of my trauma induced desperation. What I have never forgotten, however, is what happened next.

Suddenly, amid my torrent of tears, a bright light appears, enveloping me, and consuming the formerly darkened room. My face, once soaked through with tears, becomes perfectly dry. It is as if I had not spent what felt like several hours crying. A calming peace settled over me like a blanket quieting my entire body. In a flash, I realize that God Godself is with me, in that room, and that everything will be alright. I arise from the floor and climb back into bed, confident that Jesus had heard and answered my prayers. Thus begins the dance whose seeds had been sown many years prior.

I grew up in a home where the existence of God and of Jesus as God's only begotten son was a given. We attended worship regularly, but not every week, and in a variety of denominational settings (from National Baptist to United Methodist, to a non-denominational university-based fellowship, to African Methodist Episcopal, back to National Baptist, and for me, ultimately to the Episcopal Church). Believing in God and practicing that belief wherever we lived was more important than a particular denominational affiliation.

From these early childhood years, I learned the fundamentals of Christian faith, i.e., Jesus loves me this I know. I experienced a wide range of ways in which people's love and worship of God finds expression, ways that include ardent extemporaneous prayer, joyful singing, deep and abiding care for one's neighbor, sacrificial service, and the study and appropriation of Holy Scripture. The family and communities that raised me met the challenges of life with a quiet, steadfast determination to persevere.

I saw what my father did when the cupboards were bare. He would not despair. He would scramble eggs and rice together and serve up what he called egg foo young. I heard the story of how my parents responded to racial hatred when my ten-year-old brother was hit in the head with a horseshoe and the nuns at the segregated hospital refused to treat his wounds. They stood firm. They had a little talk with Jesus. They prayed as I learned to pray, simple, direct, earnest prayer that produced results. Each event, each example, deepened my awareness that God is to be found in the everyday practical exercise of human life as well as in church on Sunday mornings.

One family ritual involved traveling to Tulsa, Oklahoma, during the summers of my youth and attending annual revivals and Vacation Bible School at Mount Zion Baptist Church, one of two churches that my mother's side of the family helped found in Tulsa. Vacation Bible School is where I learned the hymn that so aptly describes my lifelong engagement with God, "I Come to the Garden Alone," and where I recall my maternal grandmother telling me, "Baby, just call on Jesus if you ever need any help. Call on Jesus." It was during a summer revival in Tulsa while I was still in my preteen years that I first publicly offered my life to Jesus and was baptized.

With my Nana, Vyola Webb Berry, church woman extraordinaire, preacher without a collar and ardent lover of Jesus, as my guide, it is not surprising that I acted upon the spiritual wisdom she provided by reaching out to Jesus in my distress. What astonished me was the personal way in which Jesus responded.

I already believed God was real but did not know it from firsthand experience. I knew God answered prayer (my Nana and my parents told me so) but had no tangible evidence of God interceding in *my* life. My relationship to God was built upon sermons and stories I had been told, books I had read, and things that happened to other people. But that paradigm shifted drastically because of my bedside encounter with God. I found out that the way God answers prayer is not limited to words on a page. God came to me as light. God generated a sense of peace that drove away my fears, dried my tears, and left me feeling deeply loved. God and Jesus became real for me in the here and now and I became open to possibilities with God that I had never considered as being applicable to me. My expectation of and experience with God were forever changed.

It would be another ten to twelve years before my ardent prayers would lead me to the revelation of God in a different manner. That decade was filled with joy and enthusiasm for God. I did not become actively involved in church, gave no thought to Christian discipleship or service, and continued to follow my family's lead when it came to where, when, and how we worshiped. I knew of God the Father and God the Son. I had little if any knowledge of and experience with the Holy Spirit. And yet I felt affirmed. I felt chosen. I talked to God regularly. Everywhere I went. My conversation was full of thanksgiving and of petition for myself and for others. I did not need a church pew or pastoral assistance. I walked in the assurance that I could go to God with anything.

Jesus and I might have stayed on this carefree path had it not been for a series of events that sent me running to the church for refuge. First a torn ligament in my left foot slowed my sometimes-frenetic roll. Then an invitation to an event where all the gathered guests were disparaging of God and of Holy Scripture started me wondering. What about me and my life, so full of private devotion and love of God, did not convey to others that I would be uncomfortable and offended by where I had been invited? I began asking of myself, "Was God alright with me as much as I thought I was alright with God?"

My questions changed from what God could do for me to what God wanted me to do for God. Prior to this shift I raised no petitions about fulfilling God's will because doing so was beyond the scope of why I was in relationship with God. I wanted and needed a Savior and a Provider. Nothing more. I was convinced that obeying the "thou shalt not" ten commandments was enough and had not conceived of the life-altering possibilities posed by God's "thou shalts." A joy-filled, effusive life of dedicated Christian service and intimacy with God was for people like my grandmother, certainly not for me.

But God desired differently. For months I prayed, listened to sermons, found myself in the audience of sermons I did not intentionally plan to hear, and talked with fellow believing seekers in the hope of hearing from God my purpose for living. The once carefree, glide-along dance of my faith journey slowed to a halt as I waited for God to tell me what God wanted me to do. This time, no light. This time no deliverance from tears. This time God's answer came in words.

You must be baptized. Feed my sheep.

Huh? I became both confused and distraught. Not by what the voice said but by what the voice meant. Had God forgotten that I had been baptized several years before? Even in my early twenties I knew the church's teaching that one baptism is sufficient (Eph 4:4–6). Besides this, I had no idea what or who God's sheep were nor what those sheep eat. The incongruity between the commandments I received and what I had grown to understand about Christianity left me doubtful as to whose voice it was that was speaking. Not unlike Nicodemus, who came to Jesus by night (John 3:1–21), and Mary, the mother of Jesus (Luke 1:26–38), I found myself asking God, "How can these things be?"

Somehow, I knew it was incumbent upon me to find out. I joined a church and eventually became director of a church-based evangelism outreach ministry. I immersed myself in what I call the Baptist version of the Anglican Alpha program, Bill Bright's *Four Spiritual Laws* and *Ten Basic Steps towards Christian Maturity*. Through these studies I was introduced to God as

Holy Spirit and Holy Scripture's teaching that the Holy Spirit is within each baptized believer as God to empower us to know and to serve God, whether we have certain experiences, like speaking in other tongues, or not. I found myself longing for the Holy Spirit to be active in my life.

I satisfied that longing by inviting the Holy Spirit to join the dance. "Come, Holy Spirit come," I prayed, "and fill me with your grace, your power, and your love." Faith not sight drove our dance until the day, while praying to God in my prayer closet, I found myself praising God in a beautiful language I did not know. The only words I could recognize were El Shaddai, the Hebrew name for God meaning "the All-Sufficient One," or "the God Who is more than enough," or "God Almighty."[2] This is the name God uses to introduce Godself to Abram (Gen 17:1) before commissioning and renaming Abram, Abraham; and to Jacob, before commissioning and renaming Jacob, Israel (Gen 35:11). Hearing that name and feeling the joy and peace that accompanied the outpouring of this new language signified to me that I was moving in the right direction.

The more I studied the Bible, attended church, and followed a discipline of prayer, worship, giving, and service, the closer I drew to God—Father, Son, and Holy Spirit. I began to trust the voice that I heard in my head, in my ears, and in my heart. It took me about a year, but I did indeed arise from the pew one Sunday morning, walked to the front of the church, and told the pastor and the church that I wanted to be baptized. Nothing else mattered. I just wanted to obey God. My relationship with God became about following Jesus (not about getting my own way or getting what I wanted) and awaiting the Holy Spirit's guidance. As I read books like Dr. Charles Stanley's *How to Listen to God*, I began to say yes to where God was leading, even when that direction resulted in painful separation and the mystery of going without knowing where. One clergy mentor commented that if I

---

2. https://stanthonyofpaduacommunity.com/parish/parish-life/ el-shaddai/#:~:text=(Hebrews%2013%3A8).,1%2C%2035%3A11).

was confident the Holy Spirit was telling me to do something, I was going to do it. And she is right.

When I began hearing a command to "come, follow me" that would mean leaving the Baptist Church I had grown to love, I first spent a couple of years arguing with God over why. It turns out God could see what I could not. When God called me to feed God's sheep, God called me to be a pastor who would empower and equip laity to serve Jesus in the church and beyond. At that time, there was little room for a single, unmarried woman to pursue that model of ministry in the Baptist Church. I finally surrendered and asked God to show me where to go. Very soon thereafter, I was meeting Episcopalians and being called an Episcopalian (to which I responded, "A what?") nearly everywhere I went. I discovered a truth. Following Jesus and obeying the Holy Spirit is not necessarily pain free. For me it meant separating from treasured friends, leaving behind a spiritual home I cherished, and foregoing a worship experience I thought I could not live without. In retrospect, moving on to start all over again in the Episcopal Church was the best decision I could have ever made.

It was also during this season of learning and growth that I adopted spiritual practices that have become a lasting part of how I experience God's presence daily and who I am as a Christian. When I awaken in the morning, for example, typically before my feet hit the floor, I thank God for being able to see a new day and I offer that day back to God. Initially I prayed a simple prayer inviting God's Holy Spirit to lead me in whatever way Jesus wanted me to go. After 9/11, I embraced the prayer of Franciscan priest Mychal Judge, a chaplain for the New York City Fire Department who lost his life on 9/11, but not before printing the words of this prayer on a card to hand out to anyone who needed it: *Lord, take me where you want me to go. Let me meet who you want me to meet. Tell me what you want me to say, and [please] keep me out of your way.*[3] On days that fall apart for no self-evident reason, I now remember what I have asked of God and thank God for whatever purpose God is using the disruption.

3. https://guideposts.org/prayer/inspirational-prayers/a-prayer-for-911/.

Since entering the Episcopal Church, my prayer life has been deeply enriched by the Book of Common Prayer and the many approaches to prayer Episcopalians pursue. I still find time to journal my conversations with God and do return to my prayer closet when times are particularly tough, but the Book of Common Prayer has provided a structure and order to praying daily that I find hard to resist. While in seminary, under the tutelage of Margaret "Peggy" Parker, I also learned how to use my passion for art as the basis for conversation with God. To stare at a piece of art and allow the Holy Spirit to bring the God connection to light, and then write a story or poem or prayer about what I see has sent me seeking God's face in ordinary as well as unexpected places, reminding me that God is everywhere and that there are no limits to when, where or how God and I can engage in conversation.

Day by day I walk in the Spirit by asking the Lord Jesus Christ to help me and the Holy Spirit to guide me. I breathe out whatever impedes my relationship with God by confessing my sins and breathe in the Holy Spirit by asking the Holy Spirit to fill me with God's light and love. Together God and I have had some amazing experiences. My first full-time position as an Episcopal priest has lasted twenty-plus years when by the guesstimates of some, it should not have lasted five. I argued with God that I was not a good fit. God's response was to keep my feet glued to the ground and my derriere glued to my seat. Be still. Be still. Be still. In twenty years, I have seen the Holy Spirit change the heart and perspective of a people, heal old wounds, bring peace where there was conflict, turn "enemies" into friends, and create a cadre of leaders whose faith in God has increased tremendously and who are unflinchingly steadfast in their determination to serve Jesus. Perhaps all that God and the people need are servants who are willing to love the people without distinction, obey the Spirit, name God's hand at work, and give God all the glory.

The Rt. Rev. Peter James Lee, twelfth Bishop of the Diocese of Virginia and the bishop who ordained me to the diaconate and to the priesthood, once preached a sermon that included this phrase: *Jesus promised those who would follow his leadings only three things: that they should be absurdly happy, entirely fearless, and always in trouble.*[4] Over the years I have learned that not everyone is ready or willing to hear the Spirit-informed truth, even when that truth is spoken in love. Going where the Spirit sends you may land you in a place where people like you have never been before. A joy-filled, effusive life of dedicated Christian service and intimacy with God may be an uncomfortable anomaly that is not well received. The beloved people of God may feel threatened by the power of God working within God's anointed, can reject the message God's Holy Spirit gives you, as well as the messenger, and out of fear, can do all manner of evil in an attempt to silence the God in you. Fortunately, years of slow dancing with God has also taught me that suffering for Christ's sake is worth it. And obeying God's commands eventually brings great reward.

Did I mention that to my knowledge, since my bedside encounter with God, my sister never again has had the excruciating headaches she had been experiencing? I may step on God's toes every now and then, and I may take back the lead that I have given over to God only to have to return it, but my prayer remains that the slow dance that God and I began during that bedside encounter will never, ever end.

Reflection, Contemplation, and Discussion Questions

1. Write down on paper who God is to you, who Jesus is to you, who the Holy Spirit is to you. Share or personally treasure what you wrote.

2. The author talks about several contemplative practices that draw her closer to God. What meditative or contemplative practices draw you closer to the Divine and/or bring you peace?

4. Attributed both to William Barclay in *The Gospel of Luke* (Presbyterian Publishing Corporation, 1956) and G. K. Chesterton. https://reformingtheline.wordpress.com/2016/01/24/no-one-would-be-more-pleased-than-g-k-chesterton/.

3. Has there been a time when your prayer or praise might have been in a "beautiful language" that was unfamiliar to you. How did that experience enhance your relationship with God?

4

God's in Me, Too

BY DIANA TURNER-FORTE, TSSF

AT TEN YEARS OLD I was already a child of order, discipline, and ritual. So, by the time my mother dispatched me at the top of a long winding staircase among other children, facing a wood door with one-way glass—anything was possible. From the other side we heard a woman's voice, rhythmic clapping, piano music, and some undecipherable sounds. There I stood trembling with terror and curiosity for entrance to my first ballet lesson, a gift bestowed on me by my parents. It turned out to be an initiation that would consume every fiber of my being.

From the moment the door opened discipline reigned. The expectations were that we respect ourselves, fellow classmates and adults, and exhibit reverence for the studio. Like my first Holy Communion—a few years earlier—entering the space procession-like, we responded accordingly. Walking as elegantly as possible on spindly legs and inflexible ballet slippers, we first acknowledged the pianist with a venerable curtsy, then proceeded to specific places at the barre awaiting the entrance of our teacher, the priestess of ceremony. Adorned in black from a wrap sweater to dance shoes with

¼-inch heels, she studied each of us with a knowing and piercing gaze. The scent of perfume and the rose that accented her severely pulled back bun softened her demeanor, somewhat.

On Saturdays when dance classes were longer and rehearsals followed—sunlight penetrated the high-ceilinged glass dome of the studio sending rays of bouncing colored crystals onto the floor as if heaven were streaming in—and I suppose it was—because dancing was an incredulously, lofty proposition—beautiful, enchanting, and holy. If in the vast universe God was truly everywhere, then I knew that God had to be in me, too. The dance studio was where I consciously encountered the divine and that symbiosis emanated through body language.

From the onset, I knew my body was where the Holy Spirit lived (1 Cor 6:19). No one told me that, neither did I take for granted that others knew the same of themselves. As I struggled with every aspect of classical ballet training from turnout to supple spine, elongated lines to graceful movements, pointe shoes to French terms; almost immediately I conceded that mastery was not likely to occur through my own volition. Mastery had to arise from a Source beyond comprehension. Therefore, I was inclined to explore the entirety of the experience with awe—to trust it, bow to it, become intimate with it, and ultimately embrace the mystery of which I dared not speak, simply because words were inadequate.

One thing was certain, dance days were special and eventually evolved into my profession, not because a teacher noticed enormous talent or I was particularly skilled at ballet, but because I was driven by that inexplicable Something I could neither relinquish or grasp which was beyond and within me. I had to dance because that was when God spoke to me.

Havelock Ellis had a distinct understanding of dance: "For dancing is the loftiest, the most moving, the most beautiful of all the arts because it is no mere translation or abstraction; it is life itself." The part of me that knew that was not logical. In my youth I had a childlike understanding that dancing was the stuff of life and God was interwoven in that, however, I was clueless as to the immensity of personal sacrifice and work needed to enliven the connection.

Mesmerized by classical ballet, I was overwhelmed by my inability to apply the instructor's corrections to my body in terms of phrasing, mood, or quality. That did not suppress my longing for the art form. The preciseness of the training kept a potent desire burning. I felt closest to God when I was saturated in sweat, out of breath from attempting a complicated *allegro*, and with an ache in my side. In spite of being wafted away by the pianist's melodic interpretations of Bach, Mozart, Tchaikovsky, Haydn and wanting to believe Jesus's quote of the psalmist: "you are gods" (John 10:34), when it came to dance I was powerless to make any alchemical application.

Regardless by the time I left home to obtain professional dance training at the Royal Winnipeg Ballet School in Canada, I knew the driving force to be divine. I was pursuing a career in which arts organizations were not inclined to welcome a person of color, much less offer employment as a dancer. The physical pain and suffocating pressure to perform held no promise of a career after my finishing school no matter how precise my lines or how good I was. I naively acquiesced to a truth that I must be an inheritor of some kind of god-current that would keep flowing. Meister Eckhart spoke to this understanding when he said: "God is a great underground river that no one can dam up and no one can stop."[1]

It appeared as though I was unstoppable. My soul knew what my body didn't and one of my tools was faith; a substance hoped for but that I was unable to see (Heb 11:1). My rudimentary tasks were to show up for lessons, work diligently, and allow grace to flow through my body as my mind frolicked with conflicting sensations simultaneously—inner joy and aching back, hips, knees, blistered feet—six hours a day. Three years of intensive training and more than a decade into the experiment, unbeknownst to me my formation had reached a pinnacle where there was no doubt that I was a classical ballet dancer in carriage, physique, and presence.

1. Dave O'Neal, *The Pocket Meister Eckhart* (Boulder, CO: Shambhala, 2018), section "Table Talk.

Shortly after that radical realization I was met by the rector at the front doors of a church I frequented. He was curious about my visits and what I was doing in Canada. When he learned I was studying classical ballet, his face beamed and he invited me to dance one Sunday for the congregation. I had no idea what he was thinking. I thought he was proposing that I perform at a church social after the worship service until he said, "Your dance will be our prayer." Even though alarmed at the prospect, I dutifully made preparations for my prayer dance, selecting music and an appropriate flowing garment designed for both movement and modesty.

On the day of my prayerful presentation, sitting beside the celebrant, my heart thumping, my mind in a whir, I heard the beginning phrases of "Morning Has Broken." Numb from sitting I stood up and presented my transmitted movement prayer. I can't tell you what happened during those mystical moments. My recollection afterward was utter stillness. A hush saturated the sanctuary and essentially absorbed the entire church like an unseasonal blanket of snow—though a bit unsure of what just happened—you didn't mind it because the sight was alluring and stunning.

The experience surpassed the ordinary and I can only say that something pressed itself upon me and allowed me to present a work of art from the depths of my newly formed body. I submit that God might have stepped in for I danced twice during that service. Another explanation might be that the classical training itself developed a physical form that had reached such a state of harmony that the divine operated without interference. For days afterward there seemed to be an afterglow and more of everything: light, joy, awareness, and vitality. Nothing was ever the same after that.

I would continue to offer danced prayers wherever I relocated as my career demanded. Consequently, for years I lived in two dancing worlds—worship services and the stage. Eventually a subtle merger occurred, as what I was given to present as my first liturgical dance, I received to dance in a theater. In the studio I was constantly struggling and striving for perfection, but in sacred settings I melded into that part of God within me—my limbs and body moving in meaningful ways on behalf of hundreds of congregations. Though not identical there was always an afterglow.

To be honest, I've never found adequate words to fully convey my prayed dance experiences. For sure, something is impressed upon me in which I am danced. I become that which I desire to be through movement. The expression exudes from a God of strength, resilience, fearlessness, and beyond all else patience. The imaginal and inspirational synchronicity stirs the vault of creativity and what emerges are devotions through an imperfect body—offerings of Spirit.

Years later when a career-threatening injury interrupted my life, trust waned as doubt made me question all that I had been receiving. During my descent into solitude, I received a different template of God in me. The grim prospects that I probably wouldn't ever dance professionally again as my legs would be too fragile to withhold the stress; thirteen fractures on my shins, not to mention the physical pain settled upon me. I wept while the doctor holding my hands delivered the life-altering news with the prescription: stay off your legs, no weight-bearing exercises, and come back in eight weeks.

In the wilderness stripped of career, income, and community and replaced with mental, physical and spiritual anguish I hung over a precipice. My life revolved around a very simple routine: a daily ritual of contrology (non-weight-bearing exercises to purify blood and sustain muscle strength), placing my hands on my shins, alternating heat and ice packs, knitting, and listening to classical music. This was my introduction to contemplation and the practice of stillness from a God of rebirth. She was empathetic, merciful, and like manna from heaven I received knowledge of self-care that was not accessible through the medical field. Her murmurings of ancient wisdom were like a soothing balm to an aching heart and wounded soul.

When I returned to the doctor's office, in silence we stared at the two sets of x-rays for what seemed like a long time. It took awhile for the distinctiveness of the x-rays to sink in. The before x-rays clearly exhibited microscopic breaks on each shin bone and beside it, after the fifty-six-day ritual, no sign of fractures. We were both in tears. Mine arose from a deep sense of gratitude and sheer relief that I had endured a trial I had not considered surmountable. The doctor admitted that he never expected the kind of recovery we were observing. There was no denying what we were seeing—affirming and redemptive moments.

In my less active state I had met the God of healing. Meister Eckhart may have well understood this when he said: "The most powerful prayer, one well-nigh omnipotent, and the worthiest work of all is the outcome of a quiet mind. The quieter it is the more powerful, the worthier, the deeper, the more telling and more perfect the prayer is. To the quiet mind all things are possible."[2] I had hosted the God of wholeness. Wandering in the desert of mystery for so long and discerning glimpses of wisdom in all that was happening was no easy task. On a much larger scale serving as a conduit for God's prayers surpassed dance in sacred settings as these embodied encounters cultivated an acute sensitivity to planetary suffering—borne humbly, silently, and contemplatively.

I'm still danced by God in the second half of life. It's an altitude I reference almost daily cloaked in the presence of the highest order, divine love. Sometimes the embodiment begins with a gentle rocking side to side, a limbering of the spine, a sustained pause on a breath, as my arms float upward, eyes softening in a reflective gaze that may or may not flow into an accelerated movement or fluid gliding around a room. And I suspect whether communally or privately, there are more embodied prayers to receive and share, more listening to do, more allowing to occur in which to revel in beauty, grace, and love until every space is hallowed.

2. Bishops Wes Frensdorff (Nevada) and Bill Gordon (Alaska), beginning in the 1950s and 1960s. A lovely account of this ethos: https://www.episcopal-church.org/sermon/sharing-frensdorffs-dream-epiphany-1-c-2013/.

Reflection, Contemplation, and Discussion Questions

1. Sometimes, life causes us to slow down or to be still. What are some things that can be gained from lessening our pace or being still?

2. The author stated she was and still is "danced by God" and gives account for both ways of being in the chapter. The author relinquished her will and body to God. What do you think it means to surrender *self*?

3. "Embodied prayer." What comes up for you? Write it down. Share or meditate privately.

5

"Stop Fighting and Know That I Am God"

BY CHARLES K. ROBERTSON

IT WAS A CLEAR June night, and in a clearing away from my camp-site, far from the lights of the city, a glance upward to the stars revealed Hercules chasing Capricorn and Pegasus across the night sky. It was a grand spectacle . . . but I was fifteen, and my personal drama prevented me from appreciating the celestial show. I cannot now recall the reason for my angst that night, which kept me from some much-needed sleep, but I will never forget what happened next. In my pocket was a paperback book of Psalms, a gift from a fellow camp counselor, a friend whose faith I admired, even if I did not understand it. I was the son of a Roman Catholic dad and a Southern Baptist mom, but my knowledge of Scripture was woefully inadequate, and any personal sense of connection I might have felt to the Divine was sorely limited.

However, with flashlight in hand, I dutifully began to read . . . and read . . . and read, until I made it through the entire Psalter. Then I went back to the beginning and started again, not sure what I was hoping to learn, but starting to feel like those words on the

39

page were speaking to me. And suddenly, I came to a halt with a single line from Psalm 46, verse 11: "Stop fighting," it declared, "and know that I am God." While I now appreciate the more poetic reading of the old King James Version—"Be still, and know"—on that summer night long ago, I needed the far more blunt wording of that modern translation. I had been struggling for some time, and did not even realize it until that moment, reading those words: "Stop fighting, and know that I am God." My response was immediate, as I answered allowed, "All right, I'll stop. Now prove it."

There was no audible reply, no angelic voices, no heavenly light. And yet, in the space of a breath, I sensed it . . . no, I knew it. I looked above, as if for the first time. Nothing had changed, and yet everything had changed. My eyes filled with tears, and I welcomed them. I welcomed all of it. In a heartbeat, the psalmist's words were real to me. I spoke aloud again, repeating words from the Apostles' Creed that I had recited countless times throughout my young life, but now truly meaning them: "I believe in one God." Yes, I now believed in one God . . . and knew that this God was there with me, above me, all around me. This knowledge was not academic, not simply assenting intellectually to a theological thesis. No, in that moment, my heart recognized beyond a shadow of a doubt that I was not alone, that I would never be alone, that God is God, and, perhaps most amazingly, that God loves me, with all my imperfections and failings. As I returned to camp, my friend (now a senior pastor in a Methodist Church) looked at me and smiled. He could sense the change in me. So, could I.

The next day, after the campout was over, I went to a store and used the money I earned to buy a study Bible, and immediately dove in, highlighting verses and writing notes in the margins. Not long after, with my parents' blessing, I joined a Bible study group for high schoolers like myself, and soon knew the books of the Bible in order and began to enjoy an eclectic group of favorites: Exodus, 1 and 2 Samuel, Isaiah, Luke and Acts, Philippians, Hebrews, and even the wild and weird book of Revelation. I was hungry to learn as much as possible.

I had always been a voracious reader, first savoring comic books and adventures by writers like Edgar Rice Burroughs and Arthur Conan Doyle, moving on to the Arthurian legends and the Shakespearean tragedies, as well as ancient history and mythology. Now I added devotions and commentaries to my list, along with works by authors previously unknown to me, like C. S. Lewis and Thomas Merton.

None of this was merely reading for the head; the words on the page jumped out at me. I quite simply could not get enough. If there was a thread of consistency in all this, it was anything that echoed the vulnerability and open questioning of those Psalms that had grabbed my heart. I was not attracted to easy answers . . . quite the opposite.

This also showed in my prayer and worship life. As I read more, I also explored what it meant to be a follower of Jesus, first within my own faith tradition and then beyond. In that formative period of my newfound faith, I visited different types of churches and dipped my toes into the charismatic experience. But I found then, as now, that what truly inspired and grounded me was being part of something larger, something with deep roots, something that linked me with so many other pilgrims who had gone before. I certainly was not going to fashion my daily life after the desert fathers and mothers of the fourth and fifth centuries . . . but I did appreciate being connected somehow to them. I had little use for joining any community that waved off two thousand years of church history.

When I prayed, when I worshiped, I wanted to do so in the company of that "great cloud of witnesses," alongside Clement of Rome, Athanasius of Alexandria, Augustine of Canterbury, Hildegard of Bingen, Bernard of Clairvaux, Francis and Clare of Assisi, Martin Luther, and all the others. (Years later, I would come to love others who in that earlier period were as yet not really known to me, including Thomas Cranmer, Dietrich Bonhoeffer, Dorothy Day, Martin Luther King, Oscar Romero.) As personal as it had become, this incredible faith could never simply be about "me and Jesus alone," but all these fellow pilgrims were now becoming part of my life, and their journeys somehow intersected with my own. And this was true not simply for all the saints of long ago. I started to realize that being a follower of Jesus meant being in community with other followers of Jesus now, in prayer, study, and worship . . . and in times of great difficulty and doubt.

All this led to my "second conversion."

I discovered the Episcopal Church in a roundabout way. I had done quite a bit of work with a parachurch group, and upon moving to a new city, I sought out the local office for that group, which just happened to be in the basement of an Episcopal church. When I asked the person there for a church recommendation, he replied, "What about upstairs?" I confess that I knew no Episcopalians and nothing about their church, beyond my vague memory of their impressive preparatory schools in the area where I grew up. Perhaps that is why I responded, "I'm not sure I would fit in." In any case, my new friend simply shrugged and said, "Why not try it out? Nothing to lose." So, I did, and as that first Sunday service came to a close, I already knew that I was home.

It wasn't long before I knew something else, and shifted my vocational plans from becoming a counselor and consultant to pursuing an ordained vocation. And this is where God stopped me in my tracks again. For a few years later, as I was walking through the church offices doing some final preparations before attending seminary, I began to turn a corner only to overhear the end of what was undoubtedly an intense and vulnerable conversation between one of the priests and the music minister. Thankfully, I stepped back before intruding, but froze in place upon hearing the priest stammer, "I'm not sure I even believe right now."

Now, I had no context for what I had just overheard, no idea of what troubles this priest was experiencing. But regrettably my immediate reaction was not one of compassion or concern, but self-righteous indignation. How could he say such a thing? I had been grilled on so many aspects of faith and liturgy and theology, and now I was about to spend three years at a seminary learning much more. Here I was, the same person who once came to faith in God because of my questions, and yet now had been spending so much time trying to learn all the answers, or as many as I could. And now I heard a senior member of the clergy say, "I'm not sure I even believe right now." How could this priest say such a thing?

Then, realizing I was still standing in place like a statue, I turned to walk away, only to hear the music minister's reply to the priest, "That's okay; for now, we'll believe for you." It hit me like a rushing wind in my face. This path of faith we've chosen to walk, this Way of Love we seek to live into . . . none of us are meant to do this journey alone. Suddenly, I remembered that while the Apostles' Creed does say, "*I* believe in one God," the Nicene Creed which I heard and proclaimed every Sunday actually says, "*We* believe in one God." I am not alone. None of us are. Not only is God present on the journey, but so are God's other beloved children.

There have been countless other experiences and epiphanies in the years since, all of which have expanded and deepened what I learned in those unexpected encounters with the Divine. God is God, so we don't have to pretend we are, not even to ourselves. "Come to me, all who are weary and heavy-laden, and I will give you rest." We are not God, but we are indeed God's beloved. As I often remind others (and myself!) now is that it is far more important what God thinks of us than what we think of God. We just need to believe, to trust God, and when we cannot even do that, we can lean on those whom God has with us on the journey, our fellow believers *and* fellow doubters. And through the fellowship we share, through the support we give to one another and to all others whom we encounter, the Spirit moves mightily, and the face of Jesus is seen once more.

Reflection, Contemplation, and Discussion Questions

1. Self-Reflection: What are you struggling with as it pertains to your faith (or lack of faith) in God? Why do you perceive there is a struggle?

2. What does the word surrender mean to you? Does the word or the act of surrender make you feel anxious?

3. Does surrender and liberation work together? If so, how? If not, why not?

6

Finding God under a Crabapple Tree

BY LINDA BEATRICE BROWN

IT STARTS WITH A storm of crabapple blossoms falling on me, surrounding me, mesmerizing with their magic and their beauty. It starts with a voice in my head that has now become as familiar as my mother's voice, and my father's voice, but is not theirs.

I still remember a day under a crabapple tree in our back yard in Akron, Ohio. I was five, maybe six, playing alone, my sisters at school. The tree was in bloom. The beauty of the blossoms was entrancing. I wanted to stay there forever. Then I heard a voice in my head saying, "You are much more than you think you are. You have something important to do. You are special." I didn't really focus on the voice. I think I wondered about it for a minute or two, and then it went out of my head. The breeze came, and a blizzard of flowers surrounded me like a fragrant snowstorm. It was total magic to my six-year-old mind. I visited the tree every day, mesmerized by the beauty until all the blossoms were blown away. This happened. Don't ask me why. I remember it like it was yesterday, not seventy-eight years ago. I never told anyone, and in my young life, it just melted into the kaleidoscope of life along with the apple blossoms. Obviously, I didn't forget it. It was lying there on a shelf in my mind, like a forgotten book in the library.

So, you might say my walk with Spirit started at six years old and has continued throughout my life. The experience with the crabapple blossoms was only the beginning. Little did I know that the "voice" that spoke to me would come back many years later when I was a fully grown woman, a mother and a teacher.

I also don't know why at seven I tried to meditate in secret, alone in a cubby in the attic. I didn't even consciously know what meditation was. My parents, while not what I would call devout Christians, were consciously moral, and what I would call spiritual seekers. They were Christian in their upbringing, and occasional churchgoers. Prayer and meditation were not part of our daily life and so I hid my impulse to do what I didn't have a name for, thinking maybe I was not supposed to be doing that.

As I grew up I forgot about my experimentation with meditation as well, until one day as an adult in a meditation workshop I remembered that I had tried a crude attempt at meditation. Oh, that's what that was! I exclaimed to myself. All I can say is that it happened and that it is part of a life following after Spirit or maybe, as some would say, the "Hounds of Heaven" have always been at my heels.

My older sister discovered that an Episcopal church was being founded in our neighborhood and she decided we should go. The two of us struck out to church together and I was confirmed at twelve years old. I was entranced and at home and loved being "churched."

Now in my eighties, I have walked with my faith in very different ways through the years, sometimes falling out of love with God, always coming back. My life with Spirit was never very far away but always there, tapping me on the shoulder when I allowed myself to temporarily shut the door to awareness.

My life was changed forever in my mid-forties. Around 1970 I discovered the world of metaphysical thought. A whole different way of thinking opened up to me. Christianity suddenly made very good sense and I discovered the New Testament through the lens of a broader understanding of universal truths. The fulcrum of this revelation was "seeing" a spirit and being startled out of my pose of cynicism by this vision. I now know that it was a gift, starting me on my lifetime spiritual journey. Understanding energy as a force, reconfigured my concept of God, and increased the longing I had to know God, to know Spirit. And this became the dominant passion of my life. I "re-discovered" the discipline of meditation and my prayer life became intensely real. The "voice" I had experienced at six in my innocence was back, and this time I paid attention, I remembered the voice, and knew it as Spirit.

Perhaps my most life-changing experience of God is the decision I made to be a devotee of Mother Mary. My experience with Mother Mary began as a result of an illness. I had always been plagued with migraines since the age of thirteen. During one particularly painful episode when I was about forty, I found myself praying and asking God for help. The answer became incredibly important to the rest of my life. I felt the presence of Spirit comforting me and I heard the "voice." When I say I "heard," it is as if in my mind, my own thinking is replaced by another source that I know as Spirit. For me this Presence often comes with words and this time It said: "Be at peace, you are not alone. We are here. You are meant to serve the sacred heart. You are meant to serve Mother Mary." I was touched, but confused and surprised. I had spent practically my whole life as an Episcopalian. What did I know about the Sacred Heart? I had not grown up in the Catholic culture, did not even know many Catholics. However, I was intrigued and also felt a tremendous pull to deepen my knowledge, pursue this message from Spirit and grow in whatever way I could in response to that "calling."

There is more to say about the following years than I can share here. I became even closer to my Episcopal roots, more assertive in my quest to learn and in my desire to follow Spirit. I began a study of metaphysics and the Wisdom Schools that is still part of my life and has enriched my connection to the teachings of Jesus. My faith is no longer what I would call one-pointed but has many facets. I came close to going to seminary. Mother Mary became my go-to figure for prayer and consolation.

However, the most profound experience of God I have ever had occurred in 2014 again during an illness. In late December 2013, I was diagnosed with breast cancer. In my shock and grief of course I went into prayer with the Mother. It was the season of Lent and I was in prayer asking for help with the cancer. I was trying to sleep when the lines of a poem began to form. I heard the entire poem in my head and wrote it down, delighted that I had been gifted with a poem. It was about Jesus. But that was the first of twenty-one poems that kept coming over the next three weeks. The poems were all from Mother Mary's point of view about the life and ministry of Jesus, the story we know so well. This was an experience of profound significance for me. I seemed to have little control over this experience. The poem about the crucifixion was completed on Easter morning after I had received it on Holy Saturday. I am afraid this writing does not do justice to this experience. I was in some ways never the same after that. For a couple of weeks I felt that I was in that "thin" place that Celtic Christianity refers to when we are very close to Spirit. Help to publish the poems and make a recording came from friends who volunteered without being asked. I felt the hand of Providence had been at work and that it was meant to happen. My faith was deepened in ways I find hard to describe. I will never forget the peace I felt during those weeks after the poems were first received by me, and the affirmation I felt for living out God's dream for me. I never present the poems in public without re-experiencing that peace. When I read the poems in public, people are often very moved and sometimes weep. Since that time my sense of being connected to and in the Presence of Spirit is totally familiar and guides my life. The voice under the crabapple blossoms is still with me. I know that I am doing the work I was meant to do with the gift of writing that I was given. I know that whatever happens I am always held in the Presence and Love of God.

Reflection, Contemplation, and
Discussion Questions

1. The author shared her experience of serving the Sacred Heart and being called to be a voice in the world of Mother Mary through poetry. Which saint has contributed to your spiritual formation? How and possibly why that particular saint?

2. Does the author's prayer invite, encourage, or give you permission to live more into a liberated life to embrace your own personal spiritual journey? If so, how?

3. The author shared her experience of God under a crabapple tree when she was six years old. When and where have you experienced Spirit's "voice" or God's presence? Why do you think God chose that particular time and location? How did it alter your life?

7

Experiencing God

Ongoing Presence and
Special Moments

BY IAN S. MARKHAM

MY SON LUKE WAS six or so. Lesley, my wife, Luke, and I were living in West Hartford, Connecticut. We worshiped as a family at Trinity Church, Hartford. Our practice with Luke was that he was allowed to take a book to church which he could read up until the start of "The Great Thanksgiving." This particular Sunday, he had a Harry Potter book with him. The exchange of the peace was finishing; and I encouraged Luke to stand on the pew and participate in the next part of the service. He put down his book and proceeded to create a circle by stretching out his arms and holding his hands together.

"What are you doing Luke? Come along stand up. The Great Thanksgiving is about to start," I said with a slightly impatient tone.

Without missing a beat, Luke just stared at me and said, "Dad, I am giving God a hug."

Luke had, even then, a strong sense of the closeness of God. In our home, God was never a big man, in the sky, that watches everything that is going on. Instead, we understood that God is in us, surrounds us, enables us to be, and is present in every situation and in every moment. Granted God is the Creator of everything that is and the cause of everything that is, but as God created so everything that is was sustained and underpinned and permeated by God.

This sense of God around me has been a part of my sense of God from my earliest memory. My experience of the world has always had this personal dimension. It is partly a sense of marvel and awe that anything is and that everything is so amazing. Color, light, thought, smells, and, in fact, all things are just incredible. But it is more than it, the world basically feels "warm." Even when I am alone, I sense an energy—which is personal—that surrounds me. And since my parents taught me that God is always with me, I have always identified this reality as God.

I don't often talk of my sense of God. I find words are stretched in my attempt to try and describe my experience in ways that sound almost unintelligible. I just used the word "energy"; and I cringe. God isn't an invisible "electricity." When talking about God, our language is metaphorical. I often resort to analogies. So, for example, imagine that you are sitting with friends in a restaurant. Let us further imagine that it is a relatively quiet evening in the restaurant. You are perhaps at a table with six or so other friends; and the conversation is relaxed, intimate, and lighthearted. Elsewhere in the restaurant, there is a young couple, perhaps on their first date, an elderly couple eating largely in silence, a family comprised of mum, dad, and two teenagers—all of whom are on their phones, and a business woman who is dining alone with an old-fashioned paper book to keep her company.

Now my experience is focused on my table. This table and our conversation are the overwhelming focus of my attention; but occasionally, I pause and notice the other diners in the restaurant. Perhaps someone at a different table gets up and heads slowly to the restroom; and for a moment I notice their attire before returning my focus to my table.

This is a little like my sense of God. My table is the lived reality of my everyday life. The other diners at the edge of my vision and consciousness are my sense of the divine life that surrounds every experience that I am having. One strength of this analogy is that it captures three elements of my experience of God: first, this pervasive warm that surrounds all my experience of the world— even when I am not looking at the other people in the restaurant I know that they are there; second, the fact that most of my focus is on the material interactions that I am having with other people and with material objects in the world because most of the time I am focused on my friends at my table; and third, there are certain moments when I truly focus on the divine, these are the moments when the other diners become the focus of my attention—when one walks passed my table. This is an analogy for my daily devotions or for the moments during a day when I pause, pray, and offer a problem or moment to God.

This ongoing presence and awareness of God isn't spectacular. It is not glossolalia. Yet it is inescapable. Over the years, I have developed certain practices that make me consciously connect with the spiritual that surrounds me. Before a difficult meeting or, at the other end of the spectrum, a fun family gathering, I will pause—tune into the energy that is surrounding me—and pray for that energy to be present in the meeting or to settle on the family gathering. It is amazing the impact that this practice has on these occasions. Meetings go better than I feared; the family gathering had a more gentle and less hectic pace.

Naturally, I interrogate myself. Is this "sense of God" just the conditioning of an extraordinarily intense religious upbringing? Is this pause before an event really just an effective mechanism of making me more attentive and present and therefore helping me function more appropriately? I concede these possibilities. Although rather than seeing them as a challenge to my theistic interpretation, I tend to think of them as perhaps the mechanisms of divine agency. So, for example, perhaps an intense religious upbringing is the training needed to discern the spiritual (and although I would not pick for others my particular journey, an intense religious upbringing can be a gift). And perhaps the prayer before events is partly answered by God through the practice of prayer itself—the fact that it leads to a more attentive Ian is God's way of answering that prayer.

The reader will note that there is a stubbornness here. The naturalistic possible explanations for my experience of God are not treated as evidence of the nonexistence of God. And, this is because there have been some "special moments" that have left me sure about the reality of a personal transcendence.

The Special Moment

My mother died on October 11, 1981. I was nineteen. It was in December 1980 that my mother noticed the dramatic swelling in her legs; and I was asked to drive her from Bodmin to Truro. It was a journey of some twenty-five miles on Cornish roads. The next eleven or so months were brutal. The cancer was everywhere. Despite various treatments, none were successful. My mother died in Hereford Country Hospital, with my father reading the Psalms to her.

The summer of 1981 was my atheist summer. I found it impossible to reconcile a loving God with the suffering of my amazing mother. I remember a special prayer meeting in the August of that year at the St. Austell Baptist Church where the congregation were praying for healing for my mother. And I remember listening to one brother who had a "Word from the Lord" that my mother would die and that God loved the distraught family. I did not appreciate that Word. The only Word I wanted was for my mother to recover and get well.

I did not behave well that summer. I drank too much (just to note—eighteen the legal drinking age). I was self-absorbed and angry. As a result, my high school performance was not strong. I failed the examinations necessary for entry to King's College London. I was forced to have a year out. I was to spend another year in Bodmin, with a grieving father and my two younger siblings, Debbie and Michael.

It was January 1982. I had retaken my "A" Levels (the exams necessary for university) and was awaiting the results. It was lunch time. I had decided to go to the pub. I made my way down the steep hill that led to the heart of the town. Passing the fifteenth-century parish church, St. Petroc's, I decided to go in. I found an empty pew and just sat there. As I did so, I cried. The pain of the loss of my mother was excruciating. Her absence was hard. For three months, that "suspended animation" feeling—I was both present but not present everywhere I went—was my daily experience. I was carrying my grief with me constantly.

As I sat there, letting the grief flood out in sobbing tears. I was aware of an intense warmth. It was a damp, cold January day—zero warmth outside and chilly inside the church. Yet the warmth was overwhelming. I felt the warmth enclose me; I felt the reassurance that I was loved; I felt a sense that mum was OK; and I knew that I could get through this.

I cannot remember how long this sensation continued. It was certainly several minutes. I remember not daring to move as the experience overwhelmed me. But finally, it dissipated. But I knew my flirtation with atheism was over. I would be a reluctant person of faith, but a person of faith I would have no choice but to be. God had decided to make himself (or herself, I am fine with either) obvious. The spiritual realm was just true: God had made sure that I knew that.

There have been other moments. When I was on a silent retreat as a student at King's College London, there was a similar moment of connection. But such moments are rare. And, to be honest, there is a side of me that is relieved that this is the case.

Standing Back

I spend most of my time in "my head." Much of my academic work has focused on "arguments" for faith. I have taken on Richard Dawkins in my *Against Atheism*;[1] I have defended the argument

1. See Ian S. Markham, *Against Atheism* (Oxford: Wiley Blackwell, 2011).

from truth to theism in *Truth and the Reality of God*.[2] I am more confident with reasons. I like a good deductive argument. The realm of feeling is opaque; I feel less sure on this territory.

Increasingly, however, I am conceding that engaging with our experience of the spiritual is important. It is perfectly possible that a supposed experience is in fact indigestion or induced by drugs. One needs to discriminate between experiences—both one's own experiences and the reports of an experience of God by others. But I suspect that there are secularists who are experiencing the spiritual and not recognizing it as such. The moment when a parent holds a newborn in their arms isn't just a natural, evolutionary sense of the miracle of life and the awareness that your genetic makeup is guaranteed to continue. The moment, for many, is so overwhelming that one is aware, if one just dare to name it, of the presence of the spiritual in this moment. The love one feels for this fragile and precious life is not just a trick of the evolutionary process to create attachment in our tribe but actually a disclosure of the divine life in the life that you are holding.

From a newborn to the sunset, these are all moments when the divine life is made real. While these spaces might be easier to see the spiritual, it is also the case that the spiritual is visible in a difficult conversation, in a moment of tragedy, and in the ugly. The Gospel of Mark reports that it was the centurion who watched the crucifixion of Jesus who finally said, "Truly this man was God's Son" (Mark 15:39).

Church should be a space where one is appropriately trained to interpret the spiritual that is all around us. Finding a way to talk about our experiences of the divine is the first and most important step in this work. We live in a spiritually-infused universe. We need to train ourselves and others to see that reality. This is our obligation as witnesses to Christ.

---

2. See Ian S. Markham, *Truth and the Reality of God: An Essay in Natural Theology* (Edinburgh: T&T Clark 1998).

Reflection, Contemplation, and
Discussion Questions

1. Reflect on a time when you decided or were moved to "pause" before or after an important situation, occasion, or event. What was the outcome of the "pause" that was of value?

2. The author shares that "we live in a spiritually-infused universe." What are your thoughts on this statement? Would you agree or disagree and why?

3. Do you agree that the church should be a space to be trained to interpret the spiritual that is all around us? If so, what would that training look like? Where would one begin?

Broad Experiences of God in Eucharist, People, and Art

8

The True Ground of My Being

BY ALTAGRACIA PEREZ-BULLARD

IT IS COMMONLY ACCEPTED by many that we live in an unenchant-ed world. Secularization and the existence of the church in a post-Christian world is regularly lamented, mostly as the cause for the loss of the worldview that made churches the center of common life, leading to the erosion of the institution. This is paired with the loss of a moral center, a knowing of right and wrong, good and evil, fur-ther eroding the social fabric, creating a moral relativism that does not fear God nor have concern for neighbors. Beneath the stated loss of faith, community, and morality lies the persistent primary concern for institutional survival for its own sake. Assumptions are made about the many benefits of religious practice. The irony is that this regret is couched in the very American pragmatism that contributes to the loss of the church primarily valuing the life of the Spirit. What might it look like if we engage in, tend to, practice our spirituality not as a resource to sustain our mental health and overall well-being, or to counteract the individualism that has left us lonely and helps us build and live in community? What if we practice spirituality in order to embed ourselves in the very heart of the Divine, engaged in a love affair that has many residual benefits, but that is a valued pursuit all on its own?

As one who survived an abusive childhood, steeped in the unmitigated impact of poverty, racism, ethnic prejudice, mental illness, addiction, sexual assault, domestic violence, homophobia, and gender discrimination, I am grateful for the gifts and hope the church provided me. Faith and the spiritual practices of prayer, fasting, Scripture study, and service were my lifeboat. A way to survive on the choppy waters of life, sometimes through ecstatic departure from the present conditions, sometimes through the emptying of self in service of others, and always through the promises of God that fed my hope that this reality was not my ultimate reality, neither in this life nor the next.

The church also contributed to my suffering and oppression, with a rigid traditionalist theology, whose patriarchy, heteronormativity, and hierarchical structure sought my conformity to a way of being human that meant erasure of the particularities of my personhood. To be embraced by their God and their community meant to deny my queerness, submit my womanhood to patriarchal authority, to leave behind my awareness of racial and ethnic marginalization and oppression, and to conform to a standard of respectability that highly valued proximity to white, middle-class, heterosexual standards of behavior, beauty, and lifestyle.

Yet my experience of God throughout my childhood was palpable and real, while ethereal and mysterious. It was more than the experience of comfort and assurance that comes from doing what is right, adhering to the tenets of faith, centering the will of God. It was a very real sense of God's presence, enveloping me, holding me, sustaining me, loving me. This absolute and complete sense that God was very real and very present has helped to define my faith and my understanding of spiritual healing and wellness. It was nurtured by the worldview and practices of my Puerto Rican community. They lived in the world keenly aware that there are forces at play, both seen and unseen, that must be navigated. Moving through the physical realm we also have present a spiritual realm, where power, strength, wisdom, and communion are accessible. Through prayer, contemplation, and worship, in community and alone, in beautiful buildings and in nature, we become aware of what is always true, that we are not alone on our journey through life, we need only tune in to God's presence. In short, my community and I live in an enchanted world.

To be with God in this way, with this understanding, is however, not exceptional, or unique. Many Black and Indigenous persons carry cultural traditions, beliefs, and practices of this type of spirituality. The understanding that God is present, always, everywhere, and that there are indications, signs, and symbols that continually call our attention to this reality, is present in many traditional religions. The cultivation of awareness, through prayer and meditation, makes these invitations to communion more easily received. My reading in African traditional religions and the practices of Indigenous peoples in the Americas strengthens and supports my Christian experiences of God as a Divine presence always present and engaged in the realities of my life. The engagement is life giving, always with the purpose of healing my brokenness, strengthening my gifts, guiding me to balance, where with tranquility and serenity I can live into the meaningful beauty that is my inheritance as a blessed, beloved child of God.

So exactly what are these experiences of God like? Comfort and tranquility when things are hard. I tangle myself up in all the things I should be doing, want to be doing, am doing, and eventually I remember to pray. As I journal or talk it out while walking, I recognize first the gift that is prayer and meditation. That I have a relationship with the Divine that welcomes me, my grief, my anxiety, my complaint, and even my resentments. The very awareness that I am praying is enough to loosen the knots of the tangle within, head, heart, and guts. I am standing with and within the Great Spirit, which shifts the way I see all that is going on. I can see a little of what God must see, and that is enough. Suddenly like a kaleidoscope, all the pretty pieces of colorful shapes shift, and I see things differently. It doesn't mean I understand everything, it just means that knowing that there is a different way to see it, I am aware of the many possibilities available in my life, the ones I can imagine and the even better ones that eventually come to be, that I could not imagine. The tension in the tangle from the pulling is loosed, the way out of the tangle becomes a little clearer. And even if there are a few false starts, where I follow a thread and it does not become loose, I am calmer and more hopeful and open that one of these strands will open the way. In this more patient space, I can now continue to explore the threads until the tangle dissolves, and I return home, or close my journal, and I am in a completely different place. I feel serenity and I am grounded in the True Ground of my Being.

Beauty and serenity surround me. I walk among the trees and water and the green, and my breath catches and then deepens. The stress is released enough to recognize the invitation to walk, to pray, to be with God. Mostly I am impressed and tickled by the creation. I wonder and delight in little bugs, in tiny wildflowers, in the chorus of singing birds. The light glistening on the ripples in the water echo Scripture, naming our God as dwelling in light in inaccessible, and indeed I cannot touch the light, but I am touched and enveloped by it. The brightness and variety of green leaves dancing in the breeze invite me to breathe, to know that the one who gave me life, breathed it into me, and that with every breath I am in the flow of the life-giving Spirit that has gifted me with life. Then I am grateful. Grateful to be walking in this Way, and then grateful for my loved ones, grateful for my ministry, grateful for the sun, or the clouds, or the wind, or the rain. The gratitude dissipates the ever-creeping resentment of things not following my rules, my direction, my control, and it turns out that it is for the best. The One who made and holds all things, inviting, teasing, guiding, is much better suited for the task.

A taste of the mystical through an altered perspective. I emerge from days on silent retreat, and everything is talking to me: the wind, the birds, the insects. I forget myself and ask God a question aloud and a gull lands in front of me and squawks, and I seem to hear God's loving response, so I follow up and the gull does too. I laugh and am delighted by this sense that like Balaam's ass, God's creatures have a prophetic word for me, that being in silence with God has allowed me to hear all of them saying Amen to the various quiet insights God has given me. I perceive all of creation engaged in a cosmic chatter about what God is doing, an experience so concrete, my attention is held, and I can absorb what God is speaking to my soul.

A call to serve through word and deed. I am grateful that my expectation of God reaching out in all manner of ways made reception of my call clear. A call confirmed in various ways but made concrete through Scripture and prayer. At fifteen, I was gathered with others at my Baptist church who accepted the invitation to be in prayer and fasting before dawn for renewal. I knelt in the pew and asked God what God would have me do with my life, to what was God calling me, asking God to speak to me through the Bible. I opened my bible and read Jer 1:4–10. I stood up from that prayer accepting, very matter-of-factly, that I was called to be an ordained minister. At another prayer service the pastor felt called to anoint my hands with oil. He may have thought it was so I could play the piano for the church. I was touched by the mystery of it, pretty clear that this clarinetist was not going to learn the piano to fill the vacancy. Years later I was moved by the confirmation of my call to serve in the Episcopal Church when this Scripture reading was offered at our priestly ordinations, and my hands were anointed by my ordaining bishop.

The joy of drums and dancing. As a priest I have many wonderful experiences of God as present in communities of worship. Singing the mass at St. Philip the Evangelist in South Central Los Angeles as we sought to bring peoples of diverse histories, cultures, classes, and languages together. A multicultural, multilingual Eucharist at Holy Faith in Inglewood, where we sang a mass setting with salsa rhythms, knowing that here was a moment that echoed eternity, the praising of God by people from many nations and tribes, peoples and tongues. Our bodies swaying, our hands clapping, the tambourines and drums accentuating that this was a feast, a fiesta indeed. The joy and ecstasy of formal worship has also been very present in informal worship. Those church moments in the early hours of the night at the Paradise Garage in New York when the life-affirming tracks, some Gospel, some World Music, most with a House beat, when with one voice we prayed with Tramaine Hawkins for the "Spirit to fall down on me." Black and brown and white bodies dancing together, people marginalized because of who they loved and their friends and allies, all feeling the freedom of Love in our midst. Those nights when the Spirit of love and justice was invoked, and we lost ourselves, for a moment, in what it means to be united for a life-giving purpose, still evoke for me the truth that the joy of the Lord is my strength (Neh 8:10). The beat of drums calls me to celebrate, to dance, to know, and to remember that in God "we live, and move, and have our being" (Acts 17:28).

I am grateful for the faith of my African and Indigenous ancestors, who knew that the Divine is very present among us. I am grateful for my Judeo-Christian ancestors, whose God of history was active for new life and freedom, especially for the poor, the marginalized, the oppressed, and the enslaved. God is very present and available. I am convinced that if we live into this truth, and proclaim it, sharing this good news, the hunger and thirst felt by many would be filled, and the church and its ministries would be vibrant. We have the message of hope that the world needs to hear. "For I am convinced that neither death, nor life . . . nor powers . . . nor anything else in all creation will be able to separate us from the of Love of God" (Rom 8:35–39). Amen.

Reflection, Contemplation, and Discussion Questions

1. In reading the author's essay, what message does Jer 1:4–10 personally convey to you?

2. The author was very transparent about her past experiences of being a survivor of oppression and suppression. In what ways can you identify with her journey and be encouraged to know that you, too, are a survivor with the help from the Divine? How has the Divine shown up for you?

3. What positive roles does multiculturalism play in your worship and social life?

9

A Food Stamp Card

BY LYDIA BUCKLIN

"How could you do that?" I asked, trying unsuccessfully to cover the wave of fear trembling in my voice.

We were new parents, our baby just eight months old. Life was full. In addition to my new role as a mother, I was working full time for the Diocese of Iowa as the Missioner for Children and Youth and enrolled in seminary, studying in the evenings for a Masters of Divinity.

As I unpacked my bags from the previous weekend's youth lock-in, my husband cooked dinner, our baby strapped to his chest.

"What was I going to do?" he asked. "It will be okay."

My husband, it turns out, had just lent some money to a family member who needed some additional funds to travel to his father who was dying in order to be with him in his final days.

I was in awe of my husband's compassion and concern *and* I was totally annoyed. It was the last $500 we had in the bank account with three weeks until our next paycheck would arrive.

Here we were, with a new baby, running out of groceries and diapers, and I must admit, I started to worry.

"Don't worry," my spouse said, "he was able to repay me."

"Oh, thank God!" I said.

"Well . . . he gave me his food stamp card."

In my privileged, sheltered life experience, I had never received public assistance. While we sometimes worried about money growing up, we always had enough. Sure, I knew plenty of people who received a food subsidy each month, but it had never been me. And the thought, I realized in that moment, was terrifying.

I took a look at the Supplemental Nutrition Assistance Program (SNAP) EBT card, issued in another person's name. What if the card didn't work? What were we even allowed to purchase? Could we get in trouble for using it?

I told my husband that he had to go buy our groceries since he was the one who had gotten us into this situation, and it turned out he wasn't so keen on the idea either. So, we made a pact to go together; we and the baby—the three of us.

"Let's just get a few things," we plotted, "to make sure the card works."

We loaded up our baby and headed to the grocery store down the street from our house. After carefully selecting our most necessary items we went to check out. Lo and behold, the card didn't work.

The cashier was extremely friendly and offered to call over the manager. Meanwhile the line was growing longer and longer. My husband felt a tap on his shoulder and an old friend from high school happened to be in the same line. The voices of the store employees grew louder as they discussed what they should do about "our situation." We left the store as quickly and discreetly as possible.

My husband called his family member, who called the state hotline and was told he needed to submit a recent pay stub to reconfirm his eligibility. The following week, after he contacted the proper office and submitted his paperwork, I decided to try again.

Only this time we really were out of food and formula. I cringed at the possibility of repeating the last attempt, so I decided to go to the place that I assumed would have plenty of experience using food assistance cards, Walmart.

I knew just how much was on the card and I knew damn well that I did not want to have to repeat this situation, so I carefully calculated the cost of each item and with my baby in tow, I headed to the check-out line.

As the older Bosnian woman provided me with the total, I slid the card and entered the pin that the card owner was *pretty sure* was the right one. Declined.

"Oh, let me try again, honey," the kind woman replied. Still declined. My heart sank. After four attempts she offered to call the manager.

"No, that's okay," I quietly said, knowing that I probably wasn't even allowed to use someone else's card. Not wanting to get in trouble, I looked at the full cart of bagged groceries, wondering how long it would take for me to put them all back on the shelves.

"I'll take care of these, dear," the kind woman replied. As my eyes filled with tears, I gently lifted my baby out of the cart and thanked her so much. I was about ten feet away when I heard her call out:

"Honey . . . can you feed your baby?"

I could no longer hold back the tears. For the first time in my life I was actually unsure how I might provide food for my family. I was embarrassed, ashamed, humbled, and broken.

Here was this woman, who I am sure made less than half of my annual salary, this woman, who, knowing other neighbors from the Bosnian community in Des Moines, most likely came to the United States for safety as a refugee. And she was reaching out to *me*. Making sure I was okay and that my baby was okay.

I could see in her eyes that she, no doubt, would have found a way to help me if I would have said, "No, we have no food."

Buddhist teacher Pema Chödrön, author of *When Things Fall Apart: Heart Advice for Difficult Times*, wrote, "When things are shaky and nothing is working, we might realize that we are on the verge of something. We might realize that this is a very vulnerable and tender place, and that tenderness can go either way. We can shut down and feel resentful or we can touch in on that throbbing quality."[1]

I must tell you that in my vulnerable, tender place I wanted to scream. I was mad at my husband and, though I tried to fight it, I found myself mad at his family member for not having "real" money to pay us back.

I was mad at a system that made using food assistance so difficult and complicated, but mostly, I was mad at myself, for letting my family get to this point, having no financial security. All I could do was worry and the anxiousness took me to a dark place where I wanted nothing more than to shut down.

But as I looked in the rearview mirror at my daughter, who had just fallen asleep, I remembered the cashier at Walmart, whose compassion and grace exceeded anything I could remember experiencing in my life.

I thought of my husband's family member, sitting at his father's bedside in his last days. A father who had abandoned his son at a young age, but who asked for one last chance at reconciliation.

And I knew we would be okay. Here I was, a minister, helper, a self-proclaimed follower of Christ. *I* was the one who was supposed to be showing the way of Jesus.

Jesus said, "The one who believes in me will do the work that I do, and will in fact do greater works than these" (John 14:12).

The cashier, who without a second thought, provided assistance to someone in need. My husband, who, if you asked him might tell you he struggles to believe in God at all.

God's truth, which has always been from the beginning, and is affirmed again by Jesus, does not call us to a life of comfort as the goal. It does not call us to a place of honor sitting on the right and left of a high king on a throne of abundance. Rather, it is a life of fulfillment.

A world where widows and orphans are cared for, the prisoners are released, the sick visited, the forgotten remembered,

---

1. Pema Chödrön, *When Things Fall Apart: Heart Advice for Difficult Times* (Boulder, CO: Shambhala, 2016), 9.

the outcasts welcomed, the workers compensated adequately, the strangers recognized, the foreigners given a home.

We make these choices in our daily lives, in our private lives, our professional lives, and our communal life. The choice to follow the way of Jesus is to truly drink from the cup. It is to remember his brokenness, his suffering, his vulnerable offering made for us.

When any one of us is bold enough and reckless enough to set out to follow him, offering ourselves for the sake of others, Jesus welcomes us.

God's Spirit comes to us in times of certainty and in times of despair. Perhaps those tender spaces of despair, worry, and disappointment actually provide just enough space for the Holy Spirit to make herself known in the compassion of a stranger.

Reflection, Contemplation, and Discussion Questions

1. How has God showed up for you as "Holy Assistance?"

2. Does the author's transparency move you to think about others' needs that are not met? In what way?

3. Meditate on the Bosnian woman (cashier) at Walmart. Write down your thoughts. How do you think she experienced God?

10

Experiencing God and Being Led by the Spirit

BY HENRY L. ATKINS JR.

AFTER ENTERING THE WORLD of the poor, stripped of all his possessions, Job has a profound experience of God. Following this experience Job says, among other things, that he has uttered what he did not understand when speaking of God. Perhaps, when we speak of our experience of God we are always, at some level, uttering what we do not understand. Yet, something there is within us which seems to urge us to speak.

The great theologian Thomas Aquinas wrote many books between 1252–1273. However, in 1273 he had a profound spiritual experience, and he never wrote another book. Aquinas entered the world of silence. He did say that his experience of God had led him to believe that all that he had written was like straw. Yet, we also know that there is a profound word about God that comes out of silence.

Job and Thomas Aquinas, among many others, remind us of the transforming nature of our experience of the God who created the heavens and the earth, and how these encounters can lead us to an awareness that all our thinking and speaking about these experiences are reflections that are always limited. Humility is a key step whenever we seek to utter what we cannot fully understand. Yet our most meaningful reflections are always on our own faith experiences, even with their limitations.

It is in the context of the profound spiritual experiences of Job and Thomas Aquinas that I write, in the hope that I may not utter what I do not understand, and that a word will emerge out of silence. A silence which has entered my heart in contemplation and taught my heart that the word that breaks forth from the heart in silence is the only word that authentically speaks to another heart.

 I want to share three experiences in this chapter. The first experience took place when I was thirteen years old. The society in which I grew up was an apartheid society, and I did not grow up in South Africa. I grew up mainly in the state of Virginia in the United States of America. In the 1950s schools were segregated, it was against the law for white people and non-white people to marry, there was almost no such thing as justice for non-whites in a court of law and every church I knew was segregated. Black people were thought of as human beings, but of a very inferior class in relation to white people.

One weekend my parents had to attend a conference. The conference was scheduled for Saturday and part of Sunday. An Afro-American woman named Mary, who had worked for our family as a maid for some years, was hired to care for me and my younger brother while my parents were at the conference.

Early Sunday morning my mother called Mary to say that the closing time of the conference had been extended to early Sunday evening, and to ask Mary if she could stay with me until around 9 p.m. My younger brother had been invited to "sleep-over" at his friend's house.

Mary informed my mother that she had to be at her church around 6:30 p.m. and would need to take me with her and would bring me home around 9:00 p.m. My mother agreed to this arrangement. Mary informed me that I would be going to church with her. I had no idea what to expect.

Around 6:30 p.m. we arrived at her church after Mary had gone to her house to change her clothes. I sat on the back pew of the small church building realizing that I had never been the only white person in an all-Black setting. Reading over the bulletin I noticed that Mary was to be a reader and that she had a last name. At least I thought it was her, and it turned out I was right. I had never though of her as a reader. As the announcements were made, I discovered that Mary taught an adult Bible class. Never had I ever thought of Mary as a teacher.

As the evening service began, I was deeply moved by the music and the spoken word. I do not remember any of the hymns or what was said in the sermon. However, during that service a "message" came very clearly to me. The message was that every person in that church was a human person just like any white person, and that God loved them in the same way that God loved me, and that I could not live anymore as if that were not true. I felt that God was speaking directly to me.

The experience changed my life. Shortly I began to experience "divine conflict" with an element of our society as the result of this divine encounter. Later in my life I would become deeply involved in the Civil Rights Movement, plan and direct many anti-racism educational events and serve as the chairperson of the Episcopal Church's National Commission on Racism, but all my racial justice ministry was based in that experience of God in that small Black Church in Virginia when I was only thirteen and the "divine conflict" is still present in my life today.

The second experience I want to relate in this chapter took place in 1981. A friend, who worked in the Latin American office of the National Council of Churches, called me in the fall of 1981 to talk about a refugee crisis in Honduras. Nearly a thousand refugees had fled a very violent conflict in El Salvador and were in living in La Virtud, Honduras, in a refugee camp on the border with El Salvador.

Reports had been coming out of the camp that Salvadoran soldiers and death-squad members were crossing over the Salvadoran border into Honduras entering the camp and taking refugees out of the camp and killing them. Some members of the staff at the National Council of Churches felt that these abuses would diminish, if some North American clergy who had had experience working in violent situations in Latin America were living in the camp, keeping watch over the camp, and confronting the intruders.

In the late 1960s I had worked as a parish priest in a very violent situation in the Dominican Republic. Our church and school were often tear gassed, soldiers often shot into our office building, and on several occasions people with whom I worked were shot and left at my office door. My friend at the National Council of Churches believed that this qualified me to be one of three clergy to be sent to live for a short period of time in La Virtud.

In the moment in which I was asked if I would be willing to go and live in La Virtud near the end of 1981 and the beginning of 1982 I felt the strong presence of the Holy Spirit. Over and over in my mind I heard/thought, "Go, I will be with you." I never doubted again that I should go.

The refugees in the camp had come out of great tribulation. Many of the female refugees had been raped. Several of the relief workers in the camp had been tortured and killed. The first woman I spoke with in the camp had seen her seventeen-year-old pregnant daughter killed by a Salvadorean soldier with his bayonet. All the refugees had left everything they had when they had to flee.

In the camp we slept on sleeping bags on the ground, ate rice and beans three times a day, drank the dirty water and confronted soldiers who came into the camp from El Salvador. We also studied the Bible in small groups and celebrated the Eucharist. Refugees often spoke of Moses, Joseph, Mary, and Jesus being refugees.

On Christmas Eve when we celebrated the "Midnight Mass" we had a dialogue sermon. One of the women who spoke told of how she had given birth to a baby in a cave while she was fleeing El Salvador. Mary, she said, had also given birth in a cave-like situation. Jesus was born in a situation not unlike the situation in which her baby was born. "This night we celebrate," she said, "with great joy that Mary, Joseph, and Jesus know our reality and are present with us."

In that moment I realized that joy was not the absence of suffering, but the gift of faith in the Incarnate One. My heart felt the joy and presence of the living God, which would enable me not only to work in La Virtud with great joy, but to continue to seek God in the refugees who live among us, and often bring with them a faith that can transform our lives here in North America.

The third experience I want to share in this chapter began with the papal encyclical *Laudate Si': On Care for Our Common Home*, written by Pope Francis in 2015. The encyclical called the universal church, and all people of good will, to embrace seven goals for the present and future well-being of the planet earth, our common home. The seven goals were a clarion call to respond to the cry of the earth, respond to the cry of the poor, develop a new form of ecological economics, the adoption of sustainable lifestyles, developing new forms of ecological education, embrace ecological spirituality, to discover God in all things, and to participate in community resilience and empowerment.

The first time I read *Laudato Si'*, in 2016, I felt that God was speaking directly to me, saying, "Do this." Over forty years ago I had served on the first Episcopal Church National Commission on Eco-Justice. In retirement I had lived for five years in a community that included Rosemary Reuther and John Cobb. I had learned a great deal from Rosemary and John about Eco-Justice. In my retirement I had also read widely in the eco-theology field, yet I was not at all sure how to respond to the call "do this."

My thoughts were drawn to the life and work of St. Francis of Assisi. I began to read more in the field of Franciscan studies, and to look for a Franciscan retreat center that was exploring *Laudato Si'*. I realized that I needed both study and prayer to clarify this call to "do this." I was led to the Holy Cross Friary and Retreat Center in Mesilla Park, New Mexico. I discovered that they were offering retreats on *Laudato Si'*. Over the next several years my wife and I attended several *Laudato Si'* and Creation Spirituality Retreats at Holy Cross. These retreats were life changing for both of us, and the meaning of "do this" was becoming clearer to me.

During one of these retreats in a conversation with Fr. Tom Smith OFM Conv., I spoke of the calling I felt in relation to *Laudato Si'*. Together, we decided that I should work with the Holy Cross Retreat Center, and the Franciscan Province of Our Lady of Consolation to coordinate their response to the *Laudato Si'* goals. In that moment I felt the Holy Spirit urging me to "do this."

"Do this" meant moving to Las Cruces, New Mexico. After some health struggles that I experienced in the fall of 2021, Treadwell (my wife) and I were able to move in March of 2022. Fr. Tom Smith OFM Conv. and I appointed a *Laudato Si'* steering committee and began a serious study of the *Laudato Si'* encyclical. We organized an ecumenical Earth Day event, which was attended by many from the larger community. We continued to offer *Laudato Si'* retreats. We have helped with letter writing campaigns to our local representatives about creation care concerns. I was able to address both the Roman Catholic and Episcopal Clergy Conferences held at the Holy Cross Retreat Center about the *Laudato Si'* goals. I also spoke to the Provincial meeting of the Franciscan Province of Our Lady of Consolation meeting at the Holy Cross Retreat Center.

The Episcopal Bishop of the Rio Grande also asked me to give the keynote address at the 2022 Diocesan convention. Immediately following the address, the bishop called for the formation of a Creation Care Committee. I rejoiced to hear from him that many people responded to his invitation.

A special blessing for me is the ecumenical nature of my new ministry. I live and work among Roman Catholics, but we reach out, following the lead of Pope Francis, to the larger faith community. People from the Orthodox, United Church of Christ, and Lutheran communities to mention a few, have been included in this new ministry. I have come to realize in a new way the importance of seeing the oneness we share in our baptism and how we can minister as one in our communities.

To experience God is to know that knowledge is love, It is to know that to live is to love, and that love leads to action. We experience this knowledge when we listen, especially in our contemplation, and become willing to walk according to the Spirit.

In my mid-eighties I am keenly aware that, especially given the serious health issues with which I live, that I am not far from having to walk through "the valley of the shadow of death," but I also know that in that valley I shall meet a guide who has been with me my whole life. I shall meet a guide who is a friend and not a stranger.

Reflection, Contemplation, and Discussion Questions

1. The author expressed that there is a profound word about God that comes out of silence. As a Christian, why is it important to meet God in the silence?

2. To obey is better than sacrifice, and to heed than the fat of rams (1 Sam 15:22). How essential is this Scripture to the Christian life?

3. What sacrifices do you think might be required to answer the call of God?

11

Finding God in People and Places

BY J. BARNEY HAWKINS IV

IN THE CHRISTIAN TRADITION, the faithful long to experience God. It is the Christian hope. Indeed, our hope comes from God, the Creator, who always longs for a new world. In God's Son, the Babe of Bethlehem, God's hope is realized for a new world which is right with God, a new heaven and a new earth. "God so loved the world, that he gave his only begotten Son, that whosoever believeth in him should not perish, but have everlasting life" (John 3:16 KJV). God's love redeems all of creation for "everlasting life" in the life, death, and resurrection of Jesus the Christ.

God's great love for the world became incarnate in Jesus, the Word made Flesh, flesh of our flesh. Jesus, the child of Nazareth, is both human and divine. The Christian Celts called such a reality a "thin place." In Jesus, heaven came to earth, so that earth could reach heaven and not "perish." "Thin places" are where the distance between heaven and earth literally collapses.

In the Holy Eucharist, we give thanks for the One who is our "experience" of God, namely Jesus the Christ. If God is "other," then Jesus of Nazareth is here and now. I dare say that my first "experience" of God was in the Great Thanksgiving of the Holy Eucharist, as found in the Book of Common Prayer, where Jesus's life, death, and resurrection have been remembered by the faithful through the ages. There at the altar in Christ Church, Greenville, South Carolina, I joined the countless throngs who have come to know the "everlasting" love of God in the Bread and Wine. The eternal meal of heaven is the here and now of earth. In the words and silence of the Holy Eucharist, I have long pondered the Divine Mystery which I will finally understand by God's grace.

Out of my experience of God in the Holy Eucharist, I was moved to journey to "thin places" where the faithful have hungered for God, as God has craved earth. My first pilgrimage was to Calcutta to work with Mother Teresa in 1983 and, subsequently in 1985. I was a searcher longing to experience God in new and deeper ways. Working with the poorest of the poor was hard work but a lasting lesson. I prayed daily to see the image of God in each suffering soul. Perhaps my most memorable "experiencing" of God in Calcutta was at the Missionaries of Charities colony for the handicapped and mentally challenged. These dear children of God were not "vegetables" but a "wealth" of God's love for a world that is unfortunately based on productivity and performance.

"Experiencing" the God whom I am always coming to know in Jesus the Christ became the reason for my subsequent pilgrimages to the Holy Land. Unintentionally but in many ways, Israel/Palestine/Holy Land has become my second home. Like the Holy Eucharist, it is a "thin place" for me, the fifth Gospel and a spiritual home where I feel connected profoundly to the Jesus of history, the Lord of my faith. Time and time again in the Basilica of the Nativity in Bethlehem, I have experienced God in the Babe of Bethlehem. I have knelt in the cave below the cluttered sanctuary at the star where tradition says Jesus was born of Mary. Here, at the center of the universe, "experiencing" God is a daily habit of so many pilgrims. I am one of them.

On so many occasions, very early in the morning and late in the afternoon, I have visited the Church of the Holy Sepulchre in the Old City of Jerusalem. Since the fourth century, this church has contained two sites that are holy to all Christians: the place where Jesus was crucified, Calvary or Golgotha; and Jesus's empty tomb or aedicule, a nineteenth-century shrine. Most pilgrims take the Via Dolorosa, the Way of the Cross, through the ancient Suk, a labyrinth of narrow streets in the Old City of Jerusalem, to reach the holiest of shrines in Christendom. Each of the fourteen Stations of the Cross points to Golgotha with the Empty Tomb nearby. A visit to the Church of the Holy Sepulchre is always tinged with sadness, as pilgrims, including I, encounter the suffering Christ of Calvary. Yet, at the Empty Tomb we meet the Risen Jesus, the Incarnate Word made flesh: very God of very God. The Church of the Holy Sepulchre is the ultimate "thin place" with all the emotions that go with being human.

"Experiencing" God is always a delight on the hill overlooking the Garden of Gethsemane and the walled Old City of Jerusalem. Here on the Mount of Olives we encounter in a twelfth-century mosque the stone which has a footprint. It is on this earthly spot, where the Tradition has it, that Jesus became the ascended Christ. The place of the Ascension is a rather bizarre interreligious site; but, holy and "other," especially for me who served for almost fourteen years as rector of the Church of the Ascension in Hickory, North Carolina.

"Experiencing" God for me has a most important and necessary subtext. While I have found God and have been found by God in the Holy Eucharist and in successive pilgrimages throughout my life, I live with ever-lingering doubts. My faith is flawed and complex with more than once the "dark night of the soul." Often, I say the Nicene Creed in the context of the Holy Eucharist with a question mark after each claim. I keep saying the Creed because it has been said for centuries. The Nicene Creed, I say, in solidarity with the faithful, more than out of personal assurance or conviction. I want to believe but I often pray, "Lord, help my unbelief."

There is, however, an "experiencing" of God which is utterly authentic and full of faith for me. It is not a liturgy or a pilgrimage to a place. It is a person. Years ago, our pediatrician and good friend broke the news. Our firstborn child had come into this world with Down syndrome and a serious heart defect. In the days and weeks and months and years that followed, I asked many questions of God. One recurrent question was simple: "What did I do wrong? How did I cause this to be?" My questions were as old as "Rabbi, who sinned, this man or his parents, that he was born blind?"

In time my wife, Linda, and I discovered that we were not the only ones to ask such questions. A friend who already journeyed for years with a severely handicapped son put it clearly. She said, "You will look in the mirror again and again always asking: 'What did I do wrong? What is wrong with me? These will be the questions of a lifetime.'" She was right. Mine is no leftover theology of long ago. My "theology" is infused with grace and questions, faith and flaws. "Experiencing" God is a questioning encounter for me. A dialogue. Our daughter, Ellen, has become the interpreter of my long, ongoing conversation with God. In Jesus, we meet the One who is real, loving, forgiving, and ever faithful. In Jesus we see the image of God in a babe, a child, a man, a Christ of Calvary, a Risen Lord, an Ascended Christ. In Ellen I have found this Jesus. She is a "thin place." She is the "wealth" that I met first in a Missionaries of Charity colony in Calcutta. I will share several vignettes which support my claim that living with Ellen is "experiencing" God.

It was Desmond Tutu, the beloved archbishop of Cape Town, who helped me to claim Ellen as a bearer of God. In the late 1980s, Tutu was the celebrant and preacher at the opening service of that year's Trinity Institute. As this small Black man in a red chasuble smiled his way down the center aisle of Trinity Church Wall Street, the whole extravagant scene became miraculously a "thin place." Suddenly, Tutu glimpsed Ellen, who was sitting on the aisle, almost dancing with delight. He stopped. He threw his arms around Ellen and proclaimed for all the world: "I can tell that you are one of the Special Ones." He surely got that right! Ellen has constantly given signs of that benediction, the good archbishop's recognition that in Ellen heaven and earth meet.

Soon after the encounter with the archbishop, the Girl Scout group in the church I was serving at the time decided that Ellen could not be in the troop—because she would not "understand" all it means to be a Girl Scout. Ellen must have been hurt—but she never showed it. Of course, her mother found another troop and Ellen seemed to "understand" it all. She certainly got serving others.

While we were living in Baltimore, I served as the rector of the Church of the Redeemer. A dear lady came to my office one day. She told me that her aunt had died in Chicago, and that she owned a beautiful mink coat. "May I give Ellen the coat? She has such style." Immediately I thought, oh the animal rights groups in Baltimore will "make hay" with this coat. Should the rector's daughter wear such an opulent garment? Linda and I discussed the gift and concluded: why not? Ellen inhabited the coat with the great style that the donor had noticed. She would saunter down the aisle of that exquisite church on Sunday morning, as though she owned the place. One Sunday, one of the church's matriarchs came up to Ellen like a "great ship coming into harbor" and said: "Ellen, that coat is lovely. It looks so real." Ellen responded: "It is real." That is Ellen. She's as real as it gets. Being "real" for Ellen had nothing to do with money or prestige or style. She loved the "real" coat that she could feel and that kept her warm. More importantly, she loved the generous lady who gave her the beautiful coat.

At the Church of the Redeemer on Christmas Eve, there was always the 5:00 p.m. Celebration of the Holy Eucharist with a live nativity scene. One year, the youth group decided that Ellen would be Mary with Patrick Ercole as Joseph. Much preparation and conversation preceded Ellen's debut as Mary. She wanted to get it just right. She took on the role of the Mother of God as though it was the most important thing she would ever do. Again, it was for her "real," not a role.

When my mother died, Ellen inherited some nice jewelry. One piece she dearly loved: pierced earrings in the shape of a diamond cross. From time to time, I would clean the earrings, soaking them in vinegar overnight. One morning as I tidied up after breakfast, I inadvertently poured the vinegar with the earrings down the drain. I felt sick to my stomach. How could I break the news to Ellen? I assumed she would be as distraught as

I: a beloved family heirloom lost forever. When she came down later that morning, we broke the news to Ellen. Without missing a best, Ellen said: "I enjoyed them while I had them." I was stunned. Forgiveness was implied. Ellen loved the earrings, not because they were valuable, but because they were her grandmother's. She did not have the earrings—but she still had memories of the grandmother she loved so much. Love and forgiveness go hand-in-glove, and that's Ellen's way of being in the world. Ellen is all about now—not what was or will be.

If Ellen is real, loving, and forgiving, she is also so often living for others. Birthdays of family and friends are always remembered, even when we might like to forget them. Ellen's devotion to her beloved aunts is legendary. She gets technology, and regular communications via Facebook assure Ellen of a community without which she could not live. Her community is close by and far afield. She speed dials with ease the Presiding Bishop of the Episcopal Church, the Most Rev. Michael Bruce Curry, to congratulate him on a "job well-done" at the royal wedding at St. George's Windsor Castle of Prince Harry and Meghan Markle. She keeps many in her orbit of care, her world of love.

Ellen's day job is working in one of the Dining Halls at Clemson University. Her gift of hospitality is real. She cleans the tables, but she also claims the hearts of some of the students who look for her cheerful, welcoming presence. Now matters.

Finally, if Ellen is real, loving, forgiving, for others and full of goodness and cheer, she is also a bold soul. This is most evident as Ellen dresses for a funeral, any funeral. No black for Miss Ellen. At the service for the Rt. Rev. Jane Holmes Dixon at the Washington National Cathedral, Ellen chose to wear a flamboyant red hat. The then Presiding Bishop, the Rt. Rev. Katharine Jefferts Shori, took great delight in Ellen's bold presence and her lively faith in the resurrected life.

Living with Ellen is an ongoing "experiencing" of God. She embodies those gifts which are surely God given. She loves lavishly. She forgives without missing a beat. She is real and authentic. She cares deeply for others. She is Christ-like without trying.

Of course, she can be stubborn and difficult. But always you know that Ellen is "wealth" untold. She is a "thin place" where heaven and earth meet.

If knowing and loving Ellen is "experiencing" God, then you might question as I do: what does she really know or understand about God and Jesus, heaven and earth? Like "who sinned this man or his parents," these questions are ones with which we must live. It is part of my conversation with God. Ellen has helped me to recognize that "experiencing" God is not an intellectual exercise or an academic endeavor. "Experiencing" the God of Ellen is not a theological study of the nature of God or religious beliefs systematically developed. The God I have come to know, with Ellen as my companion, is not about knowledge. Rather and because of Ellen, I acknowledge the Divine Mystery and give thanks that it is made real, even incarnate, in the likes of Ellen. "Experiencing" God is not a cognitive act. No, it is a recognition of God's love being in the world with us and for us. Ellen understands more than words can tell. Hers is a faith seeking an abundant life—not understanding. For me, Ellen has made "experiencing" God an encounter which is a long conversation with God, full of love and hope.

All these years later, Ellen likes to make an annual pilgrimage to the place of her baptism at Trinity Episcopal Church in Asheville, North Carolina, in 1980. Somehow, someway, by God's grace, this Child of God gets that the place where she was marked as Christ's own forever is her "thin place."

Reflection, Contemplation, and Discussion Questions

1. The author shared several of his experiences of God in a "thin place," i.e., the Eucharist, the Holy Land, daughter Ellen. What has shown to be a "thin place" for you?

2. Besides Jesus Christ, in what ways has someone else's faith walk deepened your walk with God?

3. Do you believe in the words of the Nicene Creed, Apostles Creed, and Lord's Prayer? Is there a need for more to assist your trust that these words are true?

12

In Music and in Justice

BY SANTANA ALVARADO

ONE OF MY EARLIEST memories is my mother, sister, and me sitting on the edge of my parents' bed singing *Jesus Loves Me!* Back then I would torment my sister with unending pleas for more of this sweet, simple song. I still feel the warmth and safety in those childhood memories of us singing about God's great works. The words wash over my mind, reminding me I am enough, I am loved as I am, and that my weakness is God's strength. Hymns introduced me not only to God but to the part of Godself nestled within me. Growing up it was church that played matchmaker for me and my greatest passion in life—music.

There are so many hymns living rent free in my mind. They are the soundtrack of my coming of age relationship with a Higher Power that continues to evolve. Something that drew me to the music and poetry that characterized Sunday morning was its capacity for the full spectrum of the human experience. There's enough space for the natural cycles of grief and joy, scarcity and abundance, oppression and liberation. Psalm 22 opens with, *My God, my God, why have you forsaken me?* A line I often sing in despair without relief. It's a short prayer that starts a conversation between God and I, the words carried by melody and heart.

With live music, poetry, a full script, chanting, *and* some choreography, church introduced me to the visual and performing arts, forging the creative path I faithfully follow to this day. It catalyzes my sense of purpose and has connected me with the Divine Mother, myself, and the world.

I invite you to listen to the hymn "Jesus Loves Me,"
by Anna Bartlett Warner, 1859[1]

While Sunday worship has its moments of razzle-dazzle, it was Episcopal summer camp that filled me with the Spirit. It's where I married music with intimate and intentional community. I remember struggling not to laugh through *Father Abraham Had Many Sons* in the energizing morning chapel. I remember letting the tears stream down my face as I sang the line *Spirit lead me where my trust is without borders.* Both as a camper and camp counselor, these summers were oases of spiritual experiences. The daily campfire songs sung by strangers-turned-friends taught me that faith isn't nearly as powerful if you don't share it with others. Camp isn't easy but where two or more are gathered, God is. The way we howled to the star-filled sky was proof God accepts even the silliest songs as praise.

Years later, I returned to camp as a counselor, remaining the goofy theatre kid who sang to trees. I remember one particular evening chapel. After a long day, I replaced the hymn's lyrics referring to God as "He" with "She," a little trick I picked up from my mom. The campers who overheard my creative decision laughed in shock at the change in pronouns. After chapel I explained I think it's cool that God is limitless and can reflect our unique identities because we are made in God's Image. I'm sure a little pronoun change wouldn't offend God and it allowed my full experience to shine through. I experience God as all the

---

1. Anna Bartlett Warner, "Jesus Loves Me." All Poetry. https://allpoetry.com/Jesus-Loves-Me.

possibilities and dimensions, all that is and was and will be. And like me, God is anything but one-note.

It's when I get to dream and create that God feels really alive in my life. Moments when I'm beckoned to exit society's box and meet God in the open field of uncertainty and imagination. The challenge of questioning who gets to be holy and who gets to experience God is eased by the joy I've felt welcoming my Queer, Trans, Black, Indigenous, People of Color (QTBIPOC) friends to church, after decades of their absence, to celebrate our LGBTQIA+ legacy and learn what Jesus had to say about queerness, love, and subverting empire for the marginalized.

We are created in God's image and called to create. We can pull inspiration from Spirit's artistic expression. It's in nature, people, and the extraordinary rhythms of life. Music invites me to co-create reality and include all of life's diversity when telling my story. My purpose is to spread the good news that the Trinity is alive in you as you are and that God is here, now.

I invite you to listen to the hymn "Here I Am, Lord,"
by Dan Schutte, 1981[2]

Living in Bed-Stuy, Brooklyn, trips to the deli or subway were walking meditations. The dense city air and gray concrete with polka-dotted gum stains cued it was God-time. Singing little affirmations as a way to hand whatever I was holding over to God became a habit. I would take meditation bells and create little beats to accompany the freestyles flowing from me. I would ground in the little nature New York has and remember who and whose I am. When I'm freestyling, my mouth transforms into a car and Spirit takes the wheel. I'm riding shotgun, a passenger in my own body while ancestors and angels tell stories of protection, grace, and ease.

As a Gen-Z interfaith-Episcopalian singer/songwriter my idea of fun can be a special brand of nerdy only Episcopalians know. I like to play a game where I listen to modern pop songs and

---

2. Dan Schutte, "Here I Am, Lord." Genius. https://genius.com/Dan-schutte-here-i-am-lord-lyrics.

reimagine them as spiritual devotions to God. Codependent songs about toxic relationships transform into testimonies of the ecstasy only achievable when we're close to God. Intimacy we reserve for other people becomes a space God can fill, expanding upon our desires for safety, curiosity, and acceptance. As a lover of pop music, it's important I share how I play with worldly music to serve as a reminder that nothing in this life is separate from God.

***

Mangoes falling off the trees, romantic ballads coloring the background, her smooth wrinkled skin and her attentive, listening look. The death of my grandmother, Zulma Alvarado, was the first time I really picked up the phone to the other side and asked God to put mi abuela on the line. Music is our conduit. I play Julio Jamarillo as a bat signal that I need her wisdom. I know she'll show up to help with a new recipe if I queue Los Panchos and dance around the kitchen. I had forged a relationship with mi abuela in the late stages of her life. By then Parkinson's impacted her speech. We'd sit side by side on the porch facing the familiar green Puerto Rican mountains. Her trembling fists gripped a glow-in-the-dark rosary while I recited Ave Maria. Sometimes grandpa would sit with us and say the prayers under his breath. The hot air hung around us and the mosquitos took advantage of our piety. I loved those afternoons. I love that God puts me in relationships with others knowing I will find more and more of God embedded within each of them. Shared rituals become a way to validate our shared humanity.

I always bring my guitar to my family home in Puerto Rico when visiting. Las montañas, las flores, and the family stories told by my tia on drives along the ocean inspire lyrics. I wrote a song called *La Flor de Guayanilla* for my grandma. I wanted to capture how much of a star she was to us and how she gave all of us direction. It tells the story of the flower of Guayanilla, a beautiful, eternally blooming flower people travel from all over the world to see with their own eyes. La flor de Guayanilla is the flower that never dies. I was able to play it for her during her last days in the hospital and again for our family at her wake. Songs comfort my persistent grief and remind me that music is a way to invoke the history, love, and guidance from my ancestors. I play their favorite bands and promise to never forget them, because with them I'm never alone.

I am not conflicted, I just am. I get it from the great I AM.
Who said I AM WHAT I AM. What more needs to be said?

—Santana Sankofa, BK Walking, 2022[3]

Now, I'm embarking on a new journey. I am a proud member of the board of directors for Cristosal, a human rights organization based in El Salvador, Guatemala, and Honduras. As a young person, I don't offer what a traditional board member might. I can't call up an old college friend and ask for a $50,000 check *but* I don't feel imposter syndrome because I have music. I have a kickass songwriting partner (God) and we are set on sharing Cristosal's story of hope. Human rights is the foundation for a good life. Cristosal clients and staff share a message of moving from victimhood to empowerment and suddenly everything about Daniel and the lions' den makes sense. But it's hard to constantly supply the courage to demand our right to a stable home, accessible water, education, due process, and the right to organize. I have a tool that can replenish the spirit of the people putting their bodies on the line to protect our humanity. Music has always been a way of making the weary work more tolerable. The time is now to grab the mic and speak up in solidarity with those defending God's earth, water, and people.

Songs filled with a hunger for justice fall favorably on God's ears. Proverbs 31:8–9 calls us to *open [our] mouth[s] for the mute, for the rights of all who are destitute. Open [our] mouth[s], judge righteously, defend the rights of the poor and needy.* Music isn't about escaping into the fantasy of first dates or diamonds. Music is about flipping the metaphorical table and saying capitalism, white supremacy, and trans-misogynoir have no place at the temple.

3. Santana Alvarado, "I AM." Santana Sankofa. https://www.santanasanko-fa.com.

El pájaro de libertad (bird of freedom)
Vuela por el mundo (fly around the world)
Cuenta la historia (tell the story)
Nuestra resistencia (of our resistance)

—Sin Miedo, Santana Sankofa 2023[4]

Music is my most tangible experience of God outside of my daily interactions with God's children. Music is one of my vocations on this planet and I am so thankful God trusted me enough to add my songs to the playlist for the revolution. I know God is behind it, fueling my passion to sing the same way the birds are moved by instinct to wake us up with songs every morning. It feels good and that is enough. It brings me closer to God and with God all things are possible. Even now, as a professional musician with music as my business and a form of income, it primarily serves as a hotline to God and my Ancestors. Whether it's singing at the top of my lungs with a case of cabin fever or singing in front of a crowd inviting them into the world of my album, this calling is how I truly came to see God as a partner in this life.

God is fully my momager, giving me pep talks and putting me in front of the people who need to hear my message of hope and homecoming. God is fully my ghostwriter, pulling perfect metaphors out of the ether and turning pop songs into prayers. God is fully my publicist, reminding me to be authentic because music is a practice of freeing oneself. God is fully my muse and God is fully the folds of throat tissues that form my vocal cords. When I sing I transform into the overflowing vessel God fills with Godself. *I* become an experience of God.

I invite you to listen to Whitney Houston's
"His Eye Is on the Sparrow,"
by Civilla Martin, 1905[5]

4. Santana Alvarado, "El Miedo." Santana Sankofa. https://www.santana-sankofa.com.

5. Civilla Martin, "I Sing Because I'm Happy." Timeless Truths. https://library.timelesstruths.org/music/His_Eye_Is_on_the_Sparrow/

Reflection, Contemplation, and
Discussion Questions

1. How often do you ride "shotgun" with God at the wheel of your daily life?

2. An experience with God breaks down borders we have put around God. What might cause you to "box in" the Creator?

3. Listen to or sing your favorite hymn, psalm, or spiritual song. In what ways does listening to it revive your spirit?

13

At Play in the Fields of the Lord

BY KATHARINE JEFFERTS SCHORI

I WAS BORN INTO a Roman Catholic family, my mother having grown up in that tradition, and my father in Methodism, who converted to marry my mother. Both parents lived with, and taught, a strict understanding of duty, honor, faithfulness, and right-doing. They also had an abiding yen for wilderness, and spent significant time in the mountains of the Northwest and in and around the Pacific Ocean. My siblings and I were imbued with both experiential frameworks, "walking in the Way" of godly righteousness, and soaking one's being in the awe of Creation.

At the age of five, I was sent for formation to Mesdames du Sacre Coeur, in a school for girls from first through twelfth grade. We stood when a nun or lay teacher entered the room, we curtsied when passing one in the hall, we learned French (orally and aurally in the early grades), and we were regularly counseled on our behavior—citing both flaws and achievements. Every Monday morning brought a school-wide assembly, "Prime," in which ribbons and medals were distributed for excellence during the prior week. Our report cards included numerical marks for comportment and diction and penmanship, as well as for mathematics and French. When we came to school on feast days, we changed out of our uniforms into gym suits, and played all day. There were films, treasure hunts, art projects, and special treats—all enthusiastically embraced by nuns and students. We were implicitly formed to recognize that enthusiasm derives from *en theos*, being in the presence of God, knowing the reality of God within and around us. I have fond memories of younger nuns gathering up their long black habits to run up and down the kickball field with us (this in the years before Vatican II had any local consequences).

I made my first Communion in that school community, along with quite a few other first graders, after which we shared a breakfast banquet for all the girls' families.

The Lenten discipline at school (in those days quite strict about Lent diets, fasting before going to Communion, and so on) was not so focused on denial and avoidance as it was on doing and being good, i.e., godly. I have vivid memories of the Lenten "ascent" to Easter: each girl was given a small, white plaster lamb with a ribbon around its neck bearing the girl's name. Our lambs all started at the base of a lovely wooden shelf-structure with seven stages, each smaller than the one below. Each week the lambs moved up to the next level—or not, according to the girl's behavior. I remember the time as one of heightened awareness, rather than threat. The spiritual atmosphere was always focused on greater holiness and positive growth, without debasement or psychic injury. Years after I left, I was appalled to hear stories of other religious schools using rulers on students' knuckles—or worse.

My experience in the few years I spent in that convent school was what I've long called "at play in the fields of the Lord." It was a pasture of love and grace, with wide boundaries for exploration and wonder, knowing the love of others as the grace to grow and become more like the One in whose image each creature is uniquely made.

The days and months of the school year were balanced by family excursions (even, perhaps, *pilgrimages*) to the mountains, rivers, and oceans. I remember hiking to Trout Lake when my one-year younger sister was still riding in a backpack. For me, wilderness has always been a place of solace, learning, wonder, yearning, possibility, and connection to the More. "What is this new flower, tree, bug? What makes those fascinating or eerie sounds? What makes the sky blue? What is this strange plant, with no evidence of green?" And later, "how are all of these connected," or "how have they come to be as they are?" As years went by, the questions moved toward "how can I and we care for these wonders, each one part of the community in which all living things are meant to thrive?"

My childhood was lived in the Pacific Northwest, where ocean, water, and mountains shape the weather and encourage year-round outdoor adventure. We went camping, fishing, and backpacking in all seasons, save the rare snowfall. We swam in the Sound, went crabbing and clamming at low tide, and walked the beach in all sorts of weather. At seventeen, in my first vehicle—an old VW bus, I took a half-dozen of my younger cousins to the Olympics for an overnight. We slept in a lean-to trail shelter, and woke to an elk drinking from our water bucket. A year later I hiked the higher mountain trails alone in that alpine forest, and bivouacked in the snow. The psalmist has my number: "I lift my eyes to the hills, from whence cometh my help. . . ." It's been a confirmation, rather than a question, most of my life.

Those formative years shaped a yearning for, and expectation of, connection to the whole. I'd been a fairly solitary child, deemed "different" for having been pushed ahead in school. By the time I entered a public school in the middle of fifth grade, I was two years younger than my peers. I soon learned not to share my age or history, yet eventually discovered some solidarity among the "nerds" and the girls' sports teams. Surprisingly, I found myself grounded in spite of the challenges and nastiness, knowing deep down that I was accompanied.

Walking the Way comes with excursions and seeming dead ends, as well as invitations and surprises—and seemingly *quantum* leaps. I've had several experiences of invitation to particular vocation(s). They've rarely come at my own initiative, even though for years I'd been deeply committed to studying marine communities and oceanic life (and there's some *double entendre* in that *oceanic* reference . . .). I've always been drawn to learning more, connecting more deeply, explicating and intimating the vastness of creation and its living relationality—as well as living within its relationships.

I lost the ability to continue to work as an oceanographer just as I seemed to be entering a lifetime's vocation. It was a five years' dark night of the soul. Grief, rejection, loss of identity and purpose, despair, failure . . . and yet, I found opportunities to learn things (and connections) I hadn't had the time and bandwidth to pursue. I took a year of Greek, and sat in on religious studies courses at the university. I was invited into leadership roles in my congregation, in a local women's philanthropic endeavor, in helping to draft bylaws for a new local chapter of Habitat for Humanity. I was invited to teach in the religious studies and philosophy departments. There was a lot of (gulp!) "Can I really do this?"

When the first Gulf War began in 1991, the rector invited me to preach on a Sunday when the clergy were meant to be away at a diocesan event. Who, me?! The readings included the story of Eli and Samuel, and the latter's call to listen. That experience, and nudges from several people, soon led me to say yes to seeking ordination. I was in seminary later that year. Like many others, I discovered that I had been accompanied, even in the darkness.

I still wrestled with what seemed the loss of my oceanographic vocation. At some point, I read a little book titled *Minister as Diagnostician*,[1] and began to see the connections between what I thought was lost and what stood before and around me, calling through and toward that oceanic sense of connection. Learning to look carefully at sea creatures, identifying their particular niches and gifts, as well as their location and lifeways in specific ecosystems, translated in remarkable ways to human challenges, hopes, and possibilities. That old spiritual "He's Got the Whole World in

---

1. Paul W. Pruyser, *The Minister as Diagnostician: Personal Problems in Pastoral Perspective* (Philadelphia: Westminster, 1976).

His Hands" affirms that oceanic sense of connection, all creatures bound together in the web of life and creativity.

Unexpected invitations have continued through the years, in ways that have surprised and sometimes intimidated me. After several years' work as a deacon and priest in the congregation that invited me toward ordination, I had some sabbatical time. I wanted to learn more about what was then called total ministry, but more accurately described as "ministry of all the baptized." Two highly creative leaders had spent years developing ways not only to call and equip local clergy to serve in non-traditional contexts (mostly in rural and/or indigenous congregations, largely unable to attract or fund the ministry of a priest), but also to form members of congregations as leaders and full members of the pastoral team.1 The two initiators had re-energized early church attitudes that honored the particular giftedness of all members of the community, and in many ways paved the way for the recovery of women's ordered ministry in the contemporary church. I spent some of that sabbatical time driving around the West, visiting a dozen or so congregations who were engaged in developing that ethos in a variety of contexts. I was encouraged to see the nexus of particular gifts in a specific church ecosystem, never perfect yet always seeking a healthy body of communion that fostered greater liveliness in the local, as well as larger, community.

At the end of one of those visits, the rector said to me, "What you've done here is much like what a bishop does at a visitation. We're in the process of electing a new bishop. Can I put your name in?" I laughed, heartily, and told her, "I'm a woman, I'm too young, I've never been a rector. That's ridiculous!" We had a lovely Ash Wednesday morning, and I left to drive through a snowstorm to visit a congregation in the next state. I visited in several more dioceses in the following days, and as I turned toward home, I began to feel the gravity of what that priest had asked. I arrived home on the Feast of the Annunciation, realizing that "I am only a handmaid, ready to do your bidding." It made no rational sense to me at all, but I would make the journey, wherever it led. Months later, after a week-long encounter with the people of the Diocese of Nevada, they elected me to serve as their bishop.

Leadership, leading change toward a greater Whole, is intrinsically lonely. It's also essential to fostering greater wholeness in community—to help people love one another into deeper connection. The ecosystem can only be as healthy as its members and their interactions. One of the gifts of a frontier setting is that creativity is usually honored—and the human proclivity is to enshrine or fossilize the creative chapter people are so proud of. God keeps luring us into deeper and greater connection, and human nature tends to love what *is* more than what might be. Exploring, dreaming, building connections are hard work, and change is often unwelcome. Unsettling the status quo is unpopular, even dangerous, yet it is the journey toward the heart of God.

I have been slow on the pickup many times, but I did begin to recognize the invitations. I'd been serving in Nevada for three years or so when some fellow bishops asked me if they could nominate me in the election for presiding bishop. I was shocked—and intimidated. Who, me? Again, I was too young, had only a little experience in a diocese, and I was a woman. Impossible! I wrestled, consulted, prayed, and finally acquiesced. If you need a token, I'm willing. I will walk this way, wherever it leads.

I was elected, and entered a multilingual, multinational ecosystem with immensely varied norms and expectations. Throughout the journey I have felt supported and accompanied, in time of threat and time of joy, in situations of doubt and hope, communities divided and united, individuals and systems that found me an abomination and others who became deep friends. God's ecosystem includes us all. We find the gates of heaven when we begin to see the goodness and creative possibility in each and every one of God's creatures.

Reflection, Contemplation, and Discussion Questions

1. What hymn, psalm, or music comes to your mind when out in nature?

2. Where or in what circumstances have you felt accompanied even though you were alone or in the darkness?

3. What are your thoughts around the author's statement, "Unsettling the status quo is unpopular, even dangerous, yet it is the journey toward the heart of God"? What risks are possible in disruption? What can make disruption valuable in building personal and/or community faith?

all things Bright + Beautiful
This is day Lord has made

14

Coming to Experience God through Music

By Brooks Graebner

When I was a child, I spoke like a child, I thought like a child, I reasoned like a child . . .

1 Corinthians 13:11

IN MY TEENAGE YEARS, I was drafted—drafted to play the organ for church services in the small Lutheran Church-Missouri Synod congregation where I worshiped with my family. Like any draftee, I had no clear conception of what I was getting into. The pastor who drafted me knew that I was a fairly serious student of the piano, and he asked me to step in and play the organ.

With only some rudimentary guidance from a local church organist, I commenced. Through persistence on my part and gracious forbearance on the part of the congregation, I kept that position through four years of college and over time developed some minimal competence. I never thought of myself as an organist or as someone called to a vocation in church music.

After college, when I went to divinity school and then to graduate school in religious studies, I played the organ occasionally as a substitute. And then, while still a graduate student, I stumbled into a position as organist and choir director at an Episcopal Church in Durham, North Carolina. I still did not regard myself as a church musician, but rather as someone who happened to have a skill set which made me useful to the church.

That position, however, brought me into relationship with a wonderful priest who became my mentor, and with a congregation who embraced both me and my wife in Christian community. Out of that grace-filled experience came a call to parish ministry which led me into the priesthood. Once I entered the process toward ordination, I gave up playing the organ and did not touch the instrument for thirty years.

I didn't miss playing the organ until I was nearing the end of my twenty-seven-year tenure as rector of a parish. I was blessed to have on my staff a splendid, highly accomplished organist, and as I listened to him, and as we discussed the music of the church, I began to experience a yearning to learn from him aspects of organ-playing that eluded me in my years as a largely self-taught musician.

I'm not sure what I expected to come from taking lessons in organ-playing. But I knew that I brought a very different mindset to the instrument than I had as a teenager. Now I wanted to take the time for learning the music to the best of my ability. Now I wanted to attend to the finer details of articulation and registration and technique, things which I had not done when I was younger.

But I found that it wasn't simply my relationship to organ-playing that changed; it was my relationship with God. It happened when I started to learn the *Piece d'Orgue* by J. S. Bach. This work has three sharply-contrasting sections: a single-line, toccata-like opening section that is played fast; a dense, polyphonic middle section with five interwoven lines, and an arpeggiated final section that moves chromatically to a final harmonic resolution.

> *We thank you for setting us at tasks which demand our best efforts, and for leading us to accomplishments which*

satisfy and delight us. (From *A General Thanksgiving*, The
1979 Book of Common Prayer, 836)

For someone who had given up playing the organ for decades, the effort to resume playing was demanding in and of
itself. And the demands of learning this particular composition
were considerable, especially in the middle section where nothing resolves, nothing repeats, and the five lines are constantly
moving. The learning process required considerable persistence
and repeated practice over weeks and months.

At an earlier age, I would have found myself frustrated by
the challenges. But now in retirement I found that I relished paying patient attention to the details of Bach's composition, and I
marveled at how he could spin ever-shifting patterns of dissonance
and resolution. I welcomed the opportunity to play the same mea-
sures over and over, both to address the challenges and to savor
the sounds. It was humbling and it was gratifying to trace these
patterns with my own hands and feet. And it no longer mattered
to me that it didn't come quickly or easily.

Grant to them even now glimpses of your beauty. . . .
(From the prayer *For Church Musicians and Artists*, The
1979 Book of Common Prayer, 819)

As I became more familiar and more facile with the *Piece
d'Orgue*, as the music became more and more a part of me, I
became increasingly aware of how playing it affected me, how it
stirred something deep within me.

Playing it became like embarking on a pilgrimage where I
was being guided toward a goal that I could occasionally glimpse
but not grasp; where I could sense the possibility of release and
attain it briefly, only to push forward restlessly and relentlessly. As
the second section of the piece reaches its conclusion, it grows in
intensity, but rather than reaching a definitive conclusion, it dissolves into a diminished seventh chord which leaves the listener in
suspense, wondering where the music will go next. Bach calls for
silence, refusing to let the music resolve too soon. When I played
that chord and let it resolve into silence, it called forth my deep

conviction that God is with me in the midst of doubt and uncertainty in a way that just saying those words failed to convey.

> *That we may come to those ineffable joys which thou hast prepared for those who unfeignedly love thee.* (From the collect for *All Saints' Day*, The 1979 Book of Common Prayer, 194)

Bach's answer to the unresolved chord which concludes the second section is a set of shifting six-note arpeggios that move over a descending line in the pedals. The arpeggios finally build to a flourish which resolves at last into a triumphal G major chord.

But that description in words, albeit accurate, does not capture what it means to me to play the piece and to reach the end. The triumphant resolution only comes after an arduous, labyrinthine journey, through which I must concentrate intensely and push myself physically and emotionally. I freely confess that I don't play it perfectly. But I feel God's presence, guiding and supporting me as I play the *Piece d'Orgue* in a way that no other piece evokes. I believe Bach was divinely inspired to compose it. And playing it still leaves me in awe.

Reflection, Contemplation, and Discussion Questions

1. In what ways does your life feel like a pilgrimage being guided toward a goal? Is it a challenge to grasp this image and way of being?

2. What role does the arts play in your discipleship of the Christian faith? Share which form of art transcends your faith.

3. In your opinion, is music a universal language? Why or why not?

16

Living a Resurrected Life in Love

BY RAYFORD J. RAY

CAROL CLARK WAS A local priest at Trinity Church in Gladstone. She was one of four priests who were commissioned and ordained in the 1990s. She was a retired nurse and had a deep faith and prayer life that enriched the community and the diocese. Carol Clark was the first woman president of the Standing Committee and a personal friend and actually we considered her a part of our family. As Carol aged, dementia set in and yet I always remember when she gave communion to Sue and me when she was a resident of Christian Park Village, a nursing home in Escanaba. She handed us the hosts and her very words as she handed them to us were "I love you" instead of "the body of Christ, the Bread of Heaven." I will never forget that moment because those very words "I love you" came out of her mouth as she lay dying from Covid in a nursing home. The nurse held her hand and she took her last breath at the age of ninety years. I will take that to my grave because those words came from her heart. It was her mantra in those last years of her life.

"Strength for
104 the journey"
Diana Butler Bass

At the beginning of August, we hear the story of the Transfiguration from Holy Scripture. We hear the story of Jesus revealing his glory upon a holy mountain. The disciples are awakened and developed a new way of seeing and a new way of being in this world. It is a stunning story of God revealing his presence in Jesus. It is a stunning story of God revealing his presence to humanity. Awakening all of humanity to the fact that God calls us to be aware of the presence of God in and all around us. No different when the author of the Gospel of John refers to Jesus was as the "bread of life" calling on us to be aware of God's presence in Jesus. Again, we are awakened to a new way of seeing and a new way of being in this world.

A stunning story of God revealing God's presence in this world.

When I think of Jesus as the "bread of life" I think about the living Christ here in this community. Everyone in church is a part of the body of Christ with each other and we are to connected to each other. We are in physical and spiritual relationship with each other. We are together today as the body of Christ here in this place. We are "together," all of us, the body of Christ. We can pray for one another. We can offer up acts of courage, endurance, and suffering for one another. We can support and encourage each other in good times and difficult times. We can laugh together, cry together, and love one another in this community we call the body of Christ. We, too, can know that we are part of God's salvation as we live out our lives as the living Christ here in this time and place.

Living in community I know those living and have their being will be fed by the living God in the bread and wine in the relationships that one has with each other. So that one can share that living God, *the bread of life-the love of Jesus* with others. This relationship one has with God, with Jesus with each other with humanity itself is about "love." *It is about Love received is love to be shared. It is simple and that profound.* Let me repeat that again. *It is about Love received is love to be shared. It is simple and that profound.* I believe Jesus came to show us how to be in relationship. He came to show us how to "see." Jesus came to show us how to love. Not as a King who lords his rule over his kingdom. That is not how I see Jesus nor have I ever thought of him in this manner. Our understanding of this Jesus is so much different than what was written by a writer depicting Jesus as King so many years ago. In fact, I think Jesus would have been appalled to be thought of as King. It was not who he was. The one we call Jesus came to show humanity how to receive love and share that love. He came to show us how to *live life.* It was not about power over nor about someone who sits on throne next to God. He came to reveal that everyone, can live life in its fullest. Every one of us can *experience* the Resurrection in the *"Here and Now"* if we can take down our own filters and live a life in how Jesus lived . . . and that is a life of "love." No easy task! To follow the Messiah is no easy task.

Jesus showed us how to live a new way of life. He showed us how to live in the Resurrection Now. But we have to say "Yes" to live this new way of life.

I truly believe that we "see things through our own reality." We see things through our own "filters." We may see things through anger or fear or the lens of being "right." We see things through "who we are," so saying yes to living in the Resurrection Now, to love, is no easy task.. Richard Rohr, a Franciscan priest and lecturer, says, "Most people don't see. You can't see what you are not ready to see. They don't see things as they are but see things as 'they are.' Jesus called us to a 'new way of Being.' He called us to see. He called us to be fully human and to see each other as part of the divine and to move the boundaries out where mercy, non-violence, inclusive Civility is part of living life in God. When we can do that we can 'live life' to the fullest. We know what love is actually about because it comes from here, the 'inner heart.'"[1]

To live a new way of life we must follow Jesus and how he related to humanity. Not just to worship him, but to follow. In fact, Jesus never said "worship me." He did say "come follow me." To follow Jesus meant that as a follower you had to engage your neighbor . . . you had to sit down with the Samaritans, you had

1. Richard Rohr, Center for Action and Contemplation, Daily Meditations. Found at https://cac.org/.

to eat with tax collectors, touch the leper, you had to love your neighbor. You had to widen the circle of who was in and not exclude others. You had to put yourself on the line and stretch the boundaries of inclusivity and widen God's circle of inclusion. My experience of Jesus reminds me always to include the other. I remember in Scripture where the disciples treated the man who was casting out demons as an outsider. He was not part of the inner circle and Jesus would not tolerate such behavior. He despised intolerance. As soon as Jesus heard what was going on he turned the tables on his closest followers and rebuked their blind, unbending exclusiveness. Repeatedly, Jesus' words rebuke us when we turn against others because they appear to be different. Repeatedly, the life Jesus lived and the way he taught his first disciples remind us of the expanding love of the one we know in Jesus.

To follow Jesus meant that as a follower we have to live into this way of life, a way of love, and that meant "loving God with all your heart, all your mind, and all your soul." It meant you had to treat your neighbor as yourself. To live life in its fullest you had to "love."

To follow Jesus, to know God, and to live God out is serious business. It is all about "love." It is all about relationships. It is about being the "bread of life" to each other and to this world and we are called to share it—to share the love of Christ with others so that others can be fed and live life to its fullest. Not to have hardened hearts with walls around us. Where love cannot be shared. That is not the way of Jesus. That is not the way of love.

Jesus showed us the way to live . . . a life of truth, love, justice, compassion, kindness, patience, forgiveness, and sacrifice.

We are all invited into a relationship, to the way of Jesus to the way of love. To know the God that was present at the Transfiguration. To know God as the "bread of life." To know God, present in the Jesus we know and follow. To know God in the love we have with each other—in relationships where love comes from the heart and it is to be shared.

And when Carol uttered her last breath with only the nurse being allowed to be present holding her hand, she uttered the words

"I love you" as she took her last breath. When I heard from the nurse that she said those words I wasn't surprised. In fact, it gave me goose bumps and, in all honesty, I was awakened to God, to live life in its fullest, to love once again, and the walls I put up to protect myself came tumbling down. It changed my life and I will be forever thankful to Carol Clark for mouthing three words of eternal salvation: *"I love you." Simple as that. Profound as that.*

Reflection, Contemplation, and Discussion Questions

1. When taking communion, being presented with the hosts, what thoughts come to mind? What makes communion a profound experience for you and your faith walk?

2. What Scripture or words someone has shared with you impacted your life? How has Scripture or words transformed your heart and way of being?

3. Are the words "I love you" a place of surrender?

16

Experiencing God through Liturgy

BY TIMOTHY PATTERSON

MY FIRST TRULY CONSCIOUS and direct experience of the reality of God occurred on September 22, 1974, just a few days before my twenty-second birthday. Before that, like many children I suppose, my experience of God was largely mediated by my parents, family, church, culture, and community. Raised in the Roman Catholic tradition, I was taught a conceptual idea of God as omniscient, omnipresent, and omnipotent, with all those omnis adding up to a concept that seemed generally abstract, distant, and decidedly supernatural. As a child, I do recall moments of feeling wonder and a sense of oneness with nature, though I do not remember directly associating those experiences with the God about whom I had been taught in church. However, I did experience some of the reality of God through my mother, who was deeply loving and a very devout Catholic who insisted on bringing her four children to church every Sunday, and every single day during the seasons of Lent, through all the years of our childhood. And despite the well-documented imperfections of the Roman Catholic tradition during that historical era, my mother seemed to understand intuitively the deep heart of Christian faith. Hanging on the wall of the kitchen in our home was a very 1960s mod-style plastic word sculpture which spelled the message "God Is Love." Through my mother's word and example, that message was a powerful and consistent part of my childhood experience. I will never forget one Sunday in church watching my mother praying after she had received communion, in what appeared to be a deep state of spiritual ecstasy and joy, a genuine experience of God's presence. And I remember consciously perceiving, for the first time, that there was something clearly very real and powerful going on here in this God and religion thing, at least for her. I did not fully understand it at the time, but a seed of spiritual experience was planted within me which would re-emerge and bear fruit later in life.

Through childhood, informed by my religious and family experience, I remember enjoying a general sense of cosmic safety and security. However, as adolescence and the cultural convulsions of the 1960s unfolded, religion became less and less of a vital focus for me. While I continued participating in church during those years, in all the age-appropriate programs, sacraments, classes, and groups, during my teen years and especially in the emotional wake of my parents' deteriorating marriage and eventual divorce, my subjective experience of God and church became increasingly dry, distant, abstract, and empty. When I went off to college at Duke University, realizing that there was no one really paying attention or forcing me to go at that point, I quietly dropped the habit of religion from my life.

However, at that time in the youth culture of the early 1970s, a significant interest in eastern religions began to emerge. I was particularly influenced by the teaching of Baba Ram Dass, the former Harvard professor and psychedelic explorer Richard Alpert, who had a unique voice and became an important spiritual teacher for many in my generation. Immersing myself in his book, *Be Here Now*, and recorded teachings, *Love Serve Remember*, I began to see religion in a new light to which something deep within me was drawn. I took classes in comparative religion and learned practices in yoga, meditation, and Eastern mysticism. In his teaching Ram

Dass also read extensively from the Gospel of John, and I began to wonder if there might be something more mystical and experiential to the Christ path than I had been taught in church. However, the hidden template I carried with me into my experiences of yoga and meditation was a path of "ascent." I assumed that the goal was to get up and out of the anxieties and ambiguities of the embodied human condition as I experienced it and to ascend to a higher level of consciousness. However, though I did manage to achieve some fleeting experiences of spiritual awakening and moments of inspired transcendence through my practices, I kept encountering the truth that "whatever goes up must come down." And I was unable to find an enduring experience of spiritual transformation or inner peace. Until the evening of September 22, 1974.

As I began my senior year at Duke, I found myself increasingly in the grip of anxiety and a growing sense of urgency as I faced the reality that I would soon be graduating from college and had absolutely no idea whatsoever about the vocational direction of my life. Late that afternoon, perhaps trying to flee from my emotional state, I went out for a run, got caught in a rainstorm, and returned to my apartment soaking wet. My escape route cut off and hit again by a wave of that vocational anxiety, I decided to try meditating, but, in the urgency I was feeling, the meditation turned into something more akin to an actual prayer for help. I had not prayed in that way for quite some time, but as I did I felt a quickening presence. I felt led to open the Bible on my bookshelf, which I had also not done in quite some time. Turning to the Gospel of John, I read: "And the Word became flesh and dwelt among us, full of grace and truth. . . . In him was life, and the life was the light of all people. The light shines in the darkness, and the darkness will never overcome it." And suddenly, in that moment, something broke through, not from "above," but distinctly and tangibly from "below." And in an instant I understood, in an entirely new way, the Good News of the Incarnation. I suddenly saw that it is not about getting "up and out" of the anxiety, suffering and limitation of the human condition. It is about God's light, life, and love coming "down and in" to this same human condition, to consecrate it and forever transform it. For the first time, I could feel this truth viscerally, in my body. And at that moment I consciously surrendered to God's grace and truth in Christ. I truly let it in—into the mortal flesh of my body. And, as I did, the heavy weight of that anxiety was lifted from me. I was then led to flip further through the pages, and this was one of those very Catholic devotional Bibles of that era with a section of colorful religious art in the middle. I found myself drawn to and focused on a painting of the sacred heart of Jesus. Jesus gazing directly at the viewer with this powerful light radiating out from his open heart. It sounds a bit hokey, but this is how it happened for me. As I gazed at that image, I had the physical sensation of that light-energy somehow jumping from his heart to my heart. And something very deep awakened within me. It was quite beyond words. The best I can say is that the light and love of Christ silently exploded in my heart, and radiated out to illuminate my entire being with a vivid sense of God's living presence which, since that night, I have never forgotten, never doubted and never entirely lost. I had an overwhelming sense that this is what I was made for, this is what human life is all about, and this is what the rest of my own life would be all about. The weight of all that vocational urgency was also lifted as I saw clearly that the calling of my life was to embody this divine love, to "seek first the kingdom of God," and to let the details simply work themselves out. And this has been my life path since that night and to this day.

And indeed, as the years have unfolded, the "details" since that night have largely "worked themselves out" in the context of this core commitment of my life in service to the unitive love of God. I experienced God as a living reality and a constant presence in my life, and I learned to wait in confident, increasingly patient expectation that God would indeed provide what I needed and guide me in the way I was supposed to go. That capacity for an attitude of confident, patient expectation was profoundly enhanced by my discovery of the practice of Centering Prayer as a young man working in Boston in 1975, shortly after this practice was introduced by the monks of St. Joseph's Abbey in western

Massachusetts. Along with some early exploration of conscious breathing practices, Centering Prayer provided me with a stable contemplative practice to bring mind, heart, and breath together as an integrated field of consciousness which provided a reliable means of attuning myself to God's presence, love, and guidance on a daily basis. This guidance led me to work for two years with mentally handicapped adults in Boston, to earn an MDiv degree from Duke Divinity School, to marry one of my classmates, to complete two years of clinical pastoral education, to work as a psychiatric counselor on a highly innovative inpatient unit for five years, to enter the process for ordination to the priesthood in the Episcopal Church when I finally felt called to do so, to complete two years of training in spiritual direction at General Theological Seminary in New York City, and finally to be ordained in 1989 at Holy Trinity Episcopal Church, where, to my surprise, I would serve for the next thirty years.

One might expect that my ordination would, in itself, be a peak experience of God. It was, indeed, a good and significant occasion, but it felt more like an outward event than an inward experience. For me, the goal was never to simply become a priest or become the ordained leader of a church in an institutional sense. For me, priesthood and the church were more a container and context for embodying the living and transformational reality of God's presence and inviting others into that presence. And I had become convinced that being a priest in the church would be a good way to pursue this goal. The experience of God's calling for the actual direction of my newly ordained ministry, the one that truly set me on fire, came a few months later. In September, Holy Trinity had planned a parish retreat with the Rt. Rev. Bennett Sims, who had recently retired as Bishop of Atlanta to establish the Institute for Servant Leadership. Bishop Sims's vision of servant leadership as a way of living, teaching and practicing the authentic Christ path in the real world rekindled the flame and energy of my original calling in 1974, but now with a new specificity in the paradox and practice of servant leadership. Then, just a few weeks later, I joined a group from Holy Trinity for a visit to the famous Church of the Saviour in Washington, DC, and their newly opened Servant Leadership School. And it was there that the call for my ordained ministry became crystalline in its clarity.

The Church of the Saviour was a highly innovative, ecumenical community in inner-city Washington made up of a network of small groups pursuing simultaneously the inward journey of spiritual transformation and the outward journey of radical service, gathered around a shared sense of God's call. The Servant Leadership School was designed to teach others the distilled essence of that tradition, which had given birth to an extraordinary network of inspired ministries of compassion, healing, love, and justice in that neighborhood, a manifestation of the kingdom, if you will. Along with some teaching, prayer, and meditation, we walked the streets of that inner-city neighborhood, and there we saw one incredibly powerful ministry after another, ministries of love and compassion for homeless, pregnant women, healthcare for the elderly poor, care for refugees displaced by war, for children in extreme poverty, for those in the bondage of addiction, to name a few. Ministries being done not just in the name of Christ, but being done so powerfully in the spirit of Christ, with Christ himself being a tangible presence in these ministries. Because, as they had discovered and I was now discovering, when the journey inward of faithful prayer and ever-deepening communion with God is held together with the journey outward of faithful action and life-giving service to the world, a very powerful synergy occurs which gives expression to something from beyond the merely human, namely a manifestation of the Divine. Contemplation and action. Prayer and service. Holding the two together reveals and releases the presence and power of God in our world.

Andrew Harvey speaks of two fires. The fire of the mystic—that fiery passion to live consciously in the presence and unitive love of God. That is the first fire. And the second fire is the fire of the activist, the prophet—that burning passion for embodied compassion, peace, and justice, to make the world a better place, to make God's love visible in our world, and to serve God's Dream for a world transformed. And, he says, when those two fires are

joined together, a third fire is created. That third fire has tremendous power, the power to split the atom, the power to transform
human life, the power to change the world. This is the power of
divine/human co-creation. This is the power I felt and saw fully at
work, for the first time, in the ministries of Church of the Saviour
and the Servant Leadership School. And that third fire, if you will,
split the atom of my "protective personality," what Thomas Merton
called the False Self, opened my heart in a new way, truly activated
my soul, and transformed the entire course of my ordained ministry. It was as if the scales fell from my eyes. And, for the first time,
I actually saw the body of Christ fully alive, both inwardly and
outwardly. For the first time, there on the streets of that neighborhood, I saw Jesus, really saw him, as he described himself in Matthew 25, in the faces of the least of these my brothers and sisters,
in those humble enough to serve them, in the face of every single
human being created in the image of God.

In trying to process this direct experience of Christ's living
presence with our hosts from Church of the Saviour, one of their
members, Jerry Parr, told me a story about his own ministry to
a young man living, and eventually dying, with AIDS. Jerry happened to be the Secret Service agent (the one in the trench coat)
who pushed President Reagan into the limousine after he had been
shot by John Hinckley, and is credited with saving the president's
life. Several nights a week, Jerry and his wife, a federal judge, would
bring dinner to this young man with AIDS, help him bathe, and
just spend time caring for him, loving him. One night, as he was
leaving, Jerry turned in the doorway, and instead of saying his usu-
al, "Good night, God bless you," he said to the young man, "Jesus
loves you." And without pausing a beat, the young man responded
immediately, "I love you too." For a second, Jerry thought the young
man hadn't quite heard what he said. But then, as they gazed into
one another's eyes, suddenly he realized that the young man was
looking right through Jerry. He was seeing and responding directly
to Jesus, so obviously present, alive, and at work in and through
Jerry. "Jesus loves you." "I know, Jesus. I see you, I recognize you,

and I love you too." A mutual recognition. A direct connection in the transforming power of divine love.

Teilhard de Chardin once said: "Someday, after mastering the winds, the waves, the tides and gravity, we shall harness for God the energies of love, and then, for a second time in the history of the world, man will have discovered fire." This third fire of divine/human co-creation, the joining together of contemplation and action to embody the reality of God's love in Jesus Christ, became the central, ongoing inspiration for my own ministry in Greensboro for the next thirty years.

I could offer a full recounting of the extraordinary gifts and graces of those thirty years, but that would take at least another chapter or two. Let me just say, very briefly, that I returned to Holy Trinity on fire with the call to bring this teaching and practice of the Christ path to our own community. Together with God and an ecumenical, interracial group of Christian ministers who shared this call, we co-created the Servant Leadership School of Greensboro. The school continued through my retirement and produced abundant fruits for our participants, their churches, and the larger community. I will not present a long list of these diverse manifestations of God's calling, but I will mention a couple in which I was most deeply involved personally, to give a sense of how the Spirit led me in these co-creative initiatives.

In the early 1990s, AIDS was a significant crisis for us all, but it was a particular scourge among gay men, for whom the diagnosis of AIDS was pretty much a death sentence in those days. In our community, very much in the Bible belt, these gay men with AIDS were largely ostracized, not offered much support, and were particularly wounded by their experience of rejection by their churches when they needed them most. Through conversations with some of my friends in the health care community, I had the experience of God calling me to help provide additional support, both practical and spiritual support, to persons living with AIDS, to give witness to an alternative Christian response to the reality of AIDS, and to help change the culture of Christianity in our region to a greater level of compassion, grace, and love. As an example of how these calls to specific expressions of ministry played out for me, I first felt a quickening in my body and soul which alerted me to God's active presence, I was drawn into something that felt like a field of co-creative energy, I went into a deeply receptive mode, and I was given a vision that would address the need, often in a surprising level of detail, sometimes prompting me to get a pen and paper and follow the inner urging to "Write this down!" Then I would engage and network with various people and entities who I believed might share this call. And in my experience, pretty much without exception, when it truly is the call of God, God also provides the collaborative people and the resources necessary to bring that call to manifestation. What emerged from this one was the Guilford Regional AIDS Interfaith Network (GRAIN), which gave birth to a day center providing support, caring and education for this community, which we named Higher Ground, along with a powerful county-wide network of over thirty congregation-based care teams, with the explicit structure of the inward/outward journey, which over the years richly blessed many people and families in our community living with AIDS, blessed the care-team participants in their ministries of caring for their assigned person, blessed the diversity of congregations they represented, and helped to change the whole conversation about AIDS in our region.

Another example, on Labor Day 2002, I was reflecting on the nature and value of work in the context of my growing relationships with some of the low-income people we were working with in various ways. I was slowly coming to understand some of the ways low-income people would experience what I came to call "systemic discouragement" in the ways our economy was structured. For example, even if they were working, their salaries would typically be very low, and if they were fortunate enough to be able to buy a used car, the interest rates on the auto loan would be scandalously high (far beyond what I would be charged), to the point that they were paying the actual cost of the car many times over. I visited the home of one friend in this situation and noted that she had very little furniture. Two of her sons were sharing one mattress which was on the floor, and she had rented a few pieces of furniture for her living room, with the cost of the furniture rentals being such that over time she would be paying, again, more than the retail price of this furniture many times over. Most months, she confessed to me, she had to make a choice between paying for food needed for her family and paying for the medicine she desperately needed for herself, often splitting the difference and not having enough of either. I wondered what our church and the many communities of faith in our city could do to take some pressure off the paycheck for people like this, and I felt that quickening in my body and soul. I entered the field of co-creative energy, became deeply receptive, and God gave me a very detailed vision of how, working together, the religious communities could create a small, faith-based, alternative economy of compassion and grace which, instead of "systemic discouragement," could provide at least some measure of "systemic encouragement." I was even given a name for it, The Barnabas Network, named after the biblical Barnabas, which means "son of encouragement." The vision included a large centralized warehouse that would receive donations of furniture, furnishings and appliances from people who were motivated by their faith, clients who were being served by various community agencies and ministries could be referred by the agencies to the warehouse, and those people could choose the items they wanted in something like a "shopping" experience but free of charge. Others in our community shared the sense of calling and the necessary resources appeared. The original vision also included donations of used cars for transportation to work and a jobs training program, modeled on a Church of the Saviour ministry called Jubilee Jobs. We successfully began the cars and jobs initiatives, but over time these spun off to merge with some other groups in the community with similar missions. However, The Barnabas Network as a warehouse for furniture, furnishings, and appliances continues to this day, over twenty years later, and has blessed thousands and thousands of low-income people, blessed those who have donated to it as motivated by their faith, and blessed the diversity of congregations they represent. Our

"No Child Left on the Floor" initiative alone has provided beds for thousands of children in our community.

In addition to developing and teaching the curriculum for The Servant Leadership School of Greensboro, the central focus of my ministry has been Holy Trinity Episcopal Church. All of my work at Holy Trinity has been an effort to co-create with God a community grounded in the genuine experience of God's presence. I served as assistant to the rector for the first five years of my ordained ministry. Then, when the rector announced his retirement, I found myself in a quandary. I felt a strong call to continue the work I had begun, but I was told very clearly by the bishop and diocesan authorities that I would need to move on and that, under no circumstances, could an assistant become the rector of a church they were serving. I was deeply perplexed. I went into the process of interviewing for positions at other churches, but nothing about any of them really felt right to my soul. Then, while attending a program at Kanuga Conference Center in the mountains of North Carolina, one evening in my cabin I felt particularly confused, stuck, and agitated. I decided I would pray about it once again, and I felt that familiar quickening in my body and soul. I entered the field, opened myself in receptivity. This time, instead of a vision, I was given just two words. I don't normally hear voices, but this time I heard a voice, from both beyond and within, which I identified as the voice of Christ. Two words: "Follow me." That was it. I did not know exactly what those words meant, except it seemed to be a message that I did not need to know the future, I simply needed to stay close to Jesus and he would guide me, in the present moment, in the steps I was to take. I let go of any anxiety about my future, and decided to simply follow Jesus in the moment with faith that he would guide me to the place I needed to be. I continued the interviewing process around the diocese and beyond, but six weeks later, the church and I were stunned to receive a letter from the Bishop saying that he had changed his mind and, in this one case, I would be allowed to be considered as a candidate for the rector position. Shortly after that, I was called by the search committee and vestry to become the rector of Holy Trinity. "Follow me," and that is what I continued to do.

For the next twenty-five years, the central thread of my calling was to integrate the life of a traditional, large, downtown Episcopal church with this radical, intentional, practice-based path of Christian spirituality I had come to understand through Servant Leadership. Again, in brief summary, I saw the church and the downtown city-block campus as an opportunity to co-create a network of ministries and a field of divine energy, not unlike the Church of the Saviour's neighborhood in Washington, that would bear tangible witness to the love and will of the God we were serving. Over time, inspired call by call, the church campus included the church complex itself, a spiritually innovative preschool, a music school, a youth ministry center, the Servant Leadership School and a related bookstore, a large community garden, three housing units which served as transitional homes for a significant number of refugee families from various war-torn parts of the world, a start-up location for the Mustard Seed Health Clinic providing medical care to a host of people who would otherwise not receive it, and an eleven-circuit stone labyrinth installed as a walking meditation for the entire community at the center of our church columbarium.

All of these outward manifestations flowed organically from the journey inward which was consistently nurtured through both the ministries of the church and the Servant Leadership School. The traditional spiritual practices of Episcopal liturgy, Scripture study, and Christian formation were complemented and deepened by our evolving teaching and practice of Centering Prayer, along with various breathing practices to activate the energy and intelligence of the body, the Welcoming Prayer to create contemplative space amid the activities of daily life, and a variety of other practices to support what one of the founders of Centering Prayer, Thomas Keating, called the process of Divine Therapy. The goal was to facilitate an ongoing shift of consciousness, what Jesus called metanoia, from "meta" meaning "beyond" and "nous" meaning "mind." To facilitate a shift from the relatively narrow, defensive/defending, small mind of ego, or False Self, to a consciousness that reflects the full spectrum of human intelligence, the intelligence of mind, heart, and body working together as one. This three-centered approach to Centering Prayer has a powerful way of activating the soul, opening a central channel in the temple of the body to facilitate the flow of spirit, giving expression to what Merton called True Self, unifying the whole of a person's being, and providing a tangible way of fulfilling Jesus's commandment to: Love the Lord your God with all your heart, with all your mind, with all your soul and strength.

Our liturgy, the center of the church's life, was also deeply informed by these modes of spiritual practice, and designed to invite a genuine experience of the presence of God in community. We combined a traditional Episcopal style of worship, which is powerful and glorious in itself, but deepened the experience through a rhythmic engagement with the underlying silence and a contemplative, heart-centered style of music rooted in the Taize tradition, along with selections from the Iona community and a variety of contemporary sources. The organ remained prominent, but was used more to create a rhythmic bass element in something like a richly textured "wall of sound," with the piano taking the melodic lead, complemented by evocative strings and various other instruments. The effect, especially during communion, was one of being surrounded and embraced by a spiritually activating field of musical energy that seemed to go straight to the heart and evoke a significant spiritual experience for many people. It was from that experience each week that we were sent out into the world in peace, "to love and serve you with gladness and singleness of heart, through Christ our Lord."

When I arrived at Holy Trinity the congregation numbered 1,006 members. When I retired, thirty years later, the church had grown to well over 2,500 members and had become, spiritually, a very different church. The critically important point, however, is that we were never seeking numerical growth as a goal. We were seeking spiritual growth. We were seeking the actual experience of God's living presence and the abundant fruits that flow from it.

Many people in the surrounding community who would consider themselves true "seekers," from virtually every denomination and from no denomination, found their way to Holy Trinity in those years, drawn I believe by our grounding in the genuine experience of God, in both its inward and outward expressions. Indeed, deep down, regardless of tradition, I believe that this genuine experience of God is precisely what most people who come to church are truly seeking today.

Reflection, Contemplation, and Discussion Questions

1. Who was/is a significant personal influence in your spiritual formation?

2. Reflect on a time when the Holy Scriptures seemed to illuminate your understanding in a new way. How did this illumination impact your life and the lives of others?

3. What gifts have you been given to share with others?

17

The Billy Graham Moment

BY SAMUEL S. RODMAN

I WAS LATE FOR the service, so I sat in the balcony, in the front row. I remember feeling distracted, having a hard time concentrating on the readings, and the message during the sermon seemed elusive. When it came time for communion, the balcony received first, so I made my way to the altar rail to receive the small tasteless wafer and then a sip of wine before returning to my seat above the rows of pews in the main body of the chapel.

As I knelt to pray, I found myself opening my eyes again to watch people as they made their way forward from their seats. There was a steady stream of students, faculty, and staff filling the aisle and then moving slowly, gracefully forward. I know there was music. There was always music, but no singing that morning. For the life of me, I can't remember what the organist was playing as people approached the altar.

But then something shifted, slowly, almost imperceptibly, and it felt as though everyone I recognized had received communion, but there were still people lining up, filling the aisle. And as people would return to their seats, others would come forward to receive "the body of Christ; the bread of heaven"—"the blood of Christ, the cup of salvation."

It was a steady, uninterrupted stream of people making their way forward, to receive the gifts, to be fed, to be touched, to be healed, to be filled. Time stopped altogether, but people kept coming. I didn't know where they were coming from. The numbers seemed to exceed the capacity for the chapel, and still they came. It was as though someone had opened the floodgates, or a portal, or the universe had suddenly stopped everything that it was doing and turned its full attention to our little service in a less than appealing chapel. And the whole world was making its way to our simple, sacred space.

And then, just as unexpectedly as it had begun, the moment passed, and the line dwindled down, the music softened and the servers began to assist the deacon, drawing the communion service toward it final blessing and dismissal.

I didn't tell anyone about what I had experienced, at least not right away. I only half believed it had happened at all. When I finally did share the sensation of this surreal service with a trusted friend, they asked if I had ever had an experience like this before.

My friend went on, "It sounds like a mystical moment." "What do you mean?" I asked. It sounds as though you had an experience of God in a very real and tangible way, but that others around did not have this same experience.

My friend went on to ask if there was anything else about the experience that I recalled. "Yes," I said, hesitantly, "it reminded me a bit of the Billy Graham crusades that I used to watch growing up, on the little black and white TV in my parents room."

The altar call would be given, George Beverly Shea would sing, and people began to get up from their seats to come forward. And it seemed to go on forever. People just kept leaving their seats and moving into the aisles. And it felt at times like the whole stadium full of people were making their way to the front: to pray, to surrender, to open their hearts, to offer their lives.

It felt like the feeding of the five thousand, except the people were multiplied instead of the bread and the fish. And it felt, in that moment, as though anything was possible.

This was not my first mystical experience, and it has not been my last. But it was an experience that has stayed with me more than thirty years later. It was an experience of God's spirit that opened my eyes to something that I had never seen before, and to this day cannot explain. It was an experience of the transforming power of God's promise of abundance.

It happened again, more recently, in one of our congregations. It was less intense this time, and also less disorienting, because I recognized it as it happened. I was confirming a large group of young people and adults. As I prayed for and laid hands on each person that came forward, I was focused on each one, on the promise the commitment they were making to God and to themselves. At some point I remember thinking to myself, OK, this is it, this is the whole class, and then there was another, and another, and still the rector kept calling their names and more people came forward.

At announcement time I told the congregation that they had given me what I called a "Billy Graham moment." I explained that our confirmation service is as close as we ever come, in an Episcopal service, to an altar call. But at some point what happened was less about the individuals and more about the collective sense of something unexpected unfolding. In math class it was the ancient axiom the whole was great greater than the sum of its parts. Something larger and fuller and more gracious and had gathered us together and expanded us. It was like a moment spiritual growth unfolding, and we were all caught up in it.

I tell these stories because they are connected to a biblical promise, and to a dimension of the life that is often sidestepped because it defies rational explanation, and yet, it happens. In our post enlightenment age, the mystical, transcendent experience often is met with embarrassment, confusion, and silence. But these stories are part of our journey. They are deeply connected to our relationship with the God of history, and to our identity as members of the body of Christ.

Transcendence is something we apprehend from time to time, and telling our stories is a way of bearing witness to the activities of God that we cannot fully explain, understand, nor can we dismiss them.

As we approach the end of the first quarter of the twenty-first century and emerge from a pandemic that has shaken us, as a global community and as the church, we live in a time of great anxiety. In our own particular context we find ourselves living in a world of polarization and deep confusion about what is true and what is fabrication, about who can be trusted, and about how much change we can absorb without losing our bearings completely.

In other words, we live in a time that is ripe for renewal and reform. We live in an age of great opportunity. And we can become paralyzed by our fears. More often than not our fear is connected to the idea of scarcity, that there is not enough. Not enough money, not enough food, not enough kindness, not enough compassion, not enough resources, not enough energy, not enough truth, not enough love.

Jesus is saying to us again and again, repeatedly, I am with you, there is enough, I came that you might have life and have it in abundance: All we need is here. Abundance is the promise of God we have the hardest time believing, because we are conditioned to believe the opposite. But scarcity is a lie.

When I was serving as rector of a congregation just south of Boston, in 2008, we were facing a deficit budget of $30,000. Seven people had lost their jobs. And yet there were several pressing needs that the congregation felt we were being called to respond to through relationships we has established both locally and globally. We were anxious and uncertain and we felt a clear sense that God was inviting us to respond.

We were committed to ongoing work in New Orleans as part of the long-term recovery there from Hurricane Katrina. We were inspired by the invitation of a Roman Catholic nun looking for ecumenical partners to start a school for girls in Rwanda. And one of our families needed help building an addition on their home for their son who had cerebral palsy and, as he got older and bigger, could no longer be carried to his room on the second floor.

We had no resources to meet address all of these needs and because of the economic downturn we knew not everyone would be able to meet their pledges. And yet we could not choose one of these pressing concerns over another, so we prayed, and we leaned into God's promise of abundance and we got creative and we prayed. We held fundraisers and we prayed. We shared the stories of these needs and our own commitment to these partnerships and we prayed. And we acted not out of our anxiety, but we were motivated by our love.

To this day I cannot account for how this happened, I can only tell the story. But it is a story of abundance, of grace upon grace, of the whole being more than the sum of its parts, of more and more people being drawn in and sharing in the effort to walk with our partners, to trust in the power of God's promise and to live into the gift of abundance.

At the end of the calendar year, we had made the trip to New Orleans with a team of nine people. We had made a gift to the school in Rwanda. We had raised enough money for the family to build their addition and we went from a $30,000 deficit in our budget to a $28,000 surplus. It made no sense. And yet it happened. God provided. We experienced God's promise of abundance in an unforgettable way.

The truth is, God doesn't just show up in church. The God we worship shows up on the street corner, at the local school, by the side of the road and in the local hospital ER. The gift of God's abundant presence is connected to the resurrection promise, the new life that is at the heart of Jesus gospel message. God shows up, again and again.

And we are witnesses in large and small ways to the truth of this promise. As Episcopalians, we are sometimes unsure of moments that don't seem to follow a familiar pattern. We need to remember Jesus's words to Nicodemus: that the movement of the spirit is like the wind. We don't know where it comes from, but we can see its effect, its impact.

The miracles of God's abundance can take different forms, but they have a common root. The limitless, abundant, everlasting and often surprising love of God. Each of these moments is reminder of the promise, and also foretaste of the gift that is at the heart of God's abundant love: resurrection. Mystical moments, growing in grace, faith that removes barriers are all signs and reminds of the gift that is at the center of our faith and the promise that revives and news all of us.

These little resurrections help us to empathize, embrace, and embody the resurrection that is at the heart of all that we believe. Abundance is what happens when resurrection power is unleashed in the world.

Let's share these moments. Let them lead us and guide us along the way. Let them be our witness, as well as our welcome, to any who are looking for the love of God, and open to the movement of God's Spirit. In the name of the one who shows us the fullness of God's love for each of us, Jesus.

Reflection, Contemplation, and Discussion Questions

1. The author believes "we live in a time that is ripe for renewal and reform." What does that look like for the church? What does that look like for you?

2. What kind of emotions does this essay evoke for you—hope, anxiety, anticipation, uncertainty, confidence?

3. How does prayer minimize your personal anxiety? Do you believe you are called to witness to this kind of faith? If so, how?

Made in the USA
Monee, IL
10 May 2024

58291094R00090